Journey Towards
Self Empowerment

OTHER TITLES BY EILEEN GOBLE

Spirit Guides - A Journey Through Myth to Reality
(Story of the chain of events which opened up the fascinating world of
spirit guidance and unfolding of Eileen's inner wisdom)

Gift From An Angel
(An inspirational book of channelled messages for everyday use)

White Light Meditation with Colour
(Double-sided audio-cassette plus booklet on overcoming negativity
and colour interpretation of the chakras)

Rainbow Meditation for Inner Direction and Healing
(Double-sided audio-cassette plus booklet with colour interpretations
to enhance the benefits of the meditation)

Rainbow Meditation for Change and Growth
(Double-sided audio-cassette plus booklet with colour interpretations
to enhance the benefits of the meditation)

Note: Quotes in *Journey Towards Self Empowerment* are excerpts
       from *Gift From An Angel.*

Journey Towards Self Empowerment

Eileen Goble

THE HOLISTIC CENTRE
Melbourne

Published in 1997

The Holistic Centre
55 Marianne Way,
Mt.Waverley, Vic 3149
Australia

© **Eileen Goble 1997**

Edited by Julia Wilson
Cover by Bradsworth Design

Printed in Melbourne, Australia by:
Australian Print Group

ISBN: 0 9586570 2 5
National Library of Australia

International Distributors:
Australia: Gemcraft Books Ltd, Melbourne
New Zealand: Peaceful Living Publications, Tauranga
United Kingdom: L.N. Fowler & Co. Romford, Kent

APPRECIATION

Thank you to all those who have
lovingly shared with me their hearts and
minds,
and allowed me to be a part of their
journey.

All the names used in this book have been changed to
protect the identity of the people concerned. However, I
gratefully appreciate their involvement in my life, and their
contribution to my learning and growth. It is through this
learning that I am able to share with others.

CONTENTS

1

The Power of Thought

London was being peppered with German buzz-bombs the night I was born. They were fired from France across the English Channel and just dropped out of the sky when they ran out of fuel.

Dad loved to tell the story of my mother looking out of our bathroom window and seeing one of these flying bombs in the sky and noticing the flame go out right above our house. The fright of thinking it was going to land nearby made her fall backwards into the bath. He continued the story with his familiar laugh declaring, "Eileen was born that night, the Germans sent her".

I heard that story so many times that I relegated it to one of 'dad's jokes'. However, his words were to return to me many years later, long after he had died.

Whilst studying to become a therapist I often spent time with other students developing and expanding our therapy techniques. We were working on regression therapy and my fellow student took me back to birth. I instantly became aware of being a seven year old girl, hiding in some long grass and bushes beside a railway line, looking at a little wooden railway station. It was in the country somewhere, surrounded by open space with fields and mountains in the distance. I did not recognise the scene. On the station were some German soldiers lined up with guns in their hands.

This confused me for a moment until I realised that I must have accessed a past life memory. I then became aware of feelings of doubt about some kind of decision I must make. The image I had in my mind kept repeating itself like a piece of film being played over and over again. I was a blond, blue-eyed young girl (in this life time I am dark haired with hazel eyes) and was agonising over a decision. I was looking at the soldiers on the platform and could see a train continuously moving past me. I knew I wanted to do something but was unsure of what that was.

I was explaining this to my fellow student cum 'therapist', aware that I was very conscious of being who I am in this lifetime, but also caught up in the emotions and dilemma of the young girl.

I then had a sense of running across the open space without looking in any other direction except straight ahead. I had obviously made my decision and was on the move very focused on running up the road behind the railway station. I became aware of a big black car coming up behind me and of trying to block that thought out of my mind. The image then faded.

This whole episode was both distressing and interesting. Interesting, as it was my first encounter with what must have been a past life and distressing, as I was left with the little girl's fear. I was also curious as to why the image had faded at that point.

I decided to pursue this further through my own meditations and at a later time was able to access the past life memory of the little girl hiding in the bushes. However, this time I was aware that the decision she was trying to make, was whether to stay where she was, or run across the open space behind the railway station.

I was again caught up in her indecision followed by the feeling of just running, hoping she would not get caught. I still had no idea why she was hiding or fearful of being seen.

Again, the sense of a big black car coming up behind and the childlike attempt to block this awareness out of her mind. I felt the child's panic as she was caught by a man in uniform and bundled into the car. The car drove away and the image started to fade again and I was left with a growing coldness inside, almost a sense of inevitability.

I allowed myself to go into a deeper meditative state to stay connected with the image, and once again, became aware of the little girl in the big black car. At this point I was sensing that whatever came after this was almost a *fait accompli*. The story unfolded quite quickly and I seemed to know what had happened before the time of hiding in the bushes and what would come after. It was like I was the little girl and her memory and thoughts were mine.

It appeared that my parents had been helping a Jewish family in some way. From the memory of the seven year old the facts were not clear, but they had sent me to give a message to my aunt, who lived in a neighbouring village. There seemed to be some kind of panic in the household as I left on my errand. I was also aware that they had been shot and

12

killed after I had left the house. I was on my way with the message when I was captured.

The rest was a foregone conclusion. The note I was carrying incriminated my aunt and she was picked up and we were both sent to a concentration camp. In the due course of time I was gassed. The time spent in the concentration camp is a blur and no real memories have been retained.

My immediate response to this experience was one of quite mixed emotions. It had started a train of thoughts that led to many different conclusions and assumptions. It also made a lot of sense about things that were happening in this lifetime.

My very first thought was the memory of my father's words ringing in my ears, "…the Germans sent her". Without even being consciously aware of what he was saying he had been telling me something that was fundamentally true about myself. It made me wonder about the many words that stay with us - are they also words of truth about ourselves? Are we being told in an abstract way where our past lies?

These thoughts occupied quite a deal of my time initially, then I started to realise that some of my little idiosyncrasies may have their source in that lifetime. I hate crowds and loud noises and will avoid them at all costs. As a child, I did not like having bed covers put over my head. I have to be able to breathe fresh air and prefer an open window whilst sleeping and like lots of space in my bed. I have an acute sense of smell and can detect leaking gas before most others would be aware of the smell. I dislike secrets or being privy to information that could hurt others.

I also remember that when I turned eight in this lifetime I felt a great relief, almost as if I had reached a milestone. I recall telling my mother that I was glad I was eight because now I had reached double figures. She, of course, informed me that ten was double figures but I told her I felt eight was really important. I did not know why then, but the reason for this feeling had become clear. So many things were becoming clear.

However, the thought uppermost in my mind was; why had I accessed that lifetime at a point many months before I had died? I had gone back to birth in this lifetime when the past life memory emerged. You would think that if I was accessing an immediate pre-birth memory, I would have tapped into it at a time closer to the time of death, not months prior.

Initially, it did not seem to make sense until I realised that it was at that precise moment that I virtually decided the fate of that lifetime. If I had stayed hidden and not run across the open space I would not have been caught and subsequently killed. I would still be living in what I now realised was somewhere near the German/Austrian border. I would be a little older than I am now and not an English born person living in Australia.

It was an important realisation that everything we do determines our fate. Up until that moment I could have continued with that lifetime or panicked, as I had, and died. I had total free will and there was no way that the outcome could have been predicted before I made that fateful decision. Nothing is pre-determined. Every outcome is a result of a decision whether we are consciously aware of it or not. It was a very liberating thought but one that bears great responsibility. We are totally responsible for every decision we make.

My thoughts then moved to the conclusion that I must have come back straight away, and that seemed strange, considering you would think that the mode of death would have been quite traumatic. I was also conscious of not having any great fears in this lifetime, and you would expect that if I had come back straight away, I would be carrying some trauma from that lifetime.

I decided to investigate it a little bit more and deliberately asked for guidance to help me solve what appeared to be an anomaly.

I meditated again and was instantly given an image of a little girl, sitting on the knee of a beautiful person of such light and peace, that it seemed very right for her to be there. She appeared to be quiet and subdued but the whole scene was one of solace and comfort. The little girl was receiving such loving support that she felt very safe. I realised that I was seeing her after she had gone over and was being comforted by her guides and angels.

It was so reassuring to know that she was all right and that she did not appear to be suffering. I was observing the whole scene and they seemed to be totally oblivious of my presence. I then had the impression that they were encouraging her to go back, but she was saying in a child-like voice, "I don't want to go back again, they do nasty things to you there". They continued their patient encouragement, reinforcing that she had come back before completing her task. They reminded her that she had promised to complete something. I was not sure what it was but it involved writing and at that time it was still incomplete.

She needed a lot of encouragement but finally agreed after they promised her that nothing bad would happen to her this time. She would be completely safe and they would stay with her always. I had the impression of her taking a big breath and saying, "Well, if you promise to look after me, I will go".

The image faded at that point and I was overwhelmed with a tremendous rush of love and support. I now had a deep understanding of why I had no great fears in this lifetime. I also fully understood why I was lucky enough to have beautiful loving parents who have always supported me.

What had started as a chance access to a past life during a practice session, had given me such a wonderful insight into my own spiritual nature and a deep understanding of free will and choice. I had come back straight away in human terms because I still had something to do that fitted in with the earth's present time frame. I made the decision to come back of my own free will. Admittedly, there was some persuasion, but the final choice was mine.

I have always had a deep longing to write, but when asked what it was I wanted to write, I never had an answer. Even at the time of this past life recall I still did not know that I would one day be sharing my spiritual experiences.

The final chapter of this past life recall occurred ten years later when I was invited to visit a friend in Vienna. She spent a lot of time showing me around her beautiful country. During one of these excursions we passed a little wooden railway station very similar to what I had seen in my past life recall. I was quite shocked at seeing it because that incident was far from my thoughts. I decided to tell her about that past life and my very intuitive friend invited me to visit a concentration camp that had been opened for educational purposes. I jumped at the chance to lay this ghost to rest.

She was most concerned that visiting the camp would be too traumatic and open old wounds but my first impression on walking inside the gates was that it had been sanitised. There was little left of what would have been the anguish of the inmates. I was almost distant from what must have been horrific experiences.

I visited the rooms where they slept and was told that they slept two to a bunk. The bunks were so narrow that the thought was unimaginable but it suddenly made sense of why I always needed space in my own bed.

I made a point of walking through the gas chamber and was surprised at how small it was. It then occurred to me that my image of it had been formed by the memory of a seven year old child. I then had an incredible experience; an overwhelming impression of being held in a woman's arms and being head and shoulders above everybody else. I was once again the young child and realised I must have received the gas first whilst being lovingly held in someone's arms at the time.

Perhaps my death in that lifetime was not so traumatic after all, as my last memory was one of being held lovingly and safely. Maybe I was being looked after by my loving guides and angels in that lifetime, equally as well as in this one.

The period between my first access to that past life and the visit to the concentration camp spanned over ten years, but the unfolding story fitted my growing awareness. I received the information when I was best able to assimilate the message and when it was right for my growth.

I also realised that every lifetime is an opportunity to grow and learn and that we do not have to bring one life's traumas into another. The whole experience added to my growing understanding of the power, thought, has on our reality. Our decisions are based on our thoughts at any given time and our thoughts are influenced by our emotional state at that time.

The little girl's decision to run was based on her conscious thoughts, influenced by her age and emotional state. Looking at her decision one could be forgiven for thinking she had made a mistake and therefore ended up being killed. However, in reality, her decision just altered the outcome slightly. I did come back and, apart from a slight geographical relocation, am presumably back on track doing what was intended in the first place.

If her experience is anything to go by then we do not make mistakes, just decisions. This is one of the things I have come to understand very well, not only from that experience, but also through the many clients and students I have helped over the years.

That first past life experience started me on a journey of understanding the power of thought. I have travelled far on that journey, opening up my awareness to the wide and varied ways in which we use our decision making process.

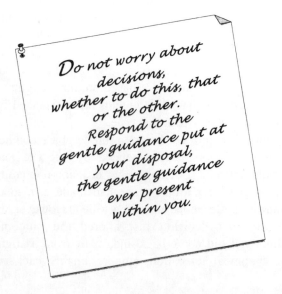

Do not worry about decisions, whether to do this, that or the other.
Respond to the gentle guidance put at your disposal, the gentle guidance ever present within you.

2

Making Decisions

I was working on my computer one day and it occurred to me that our minds seem to operate along very similar lines. We input information, store it away and retrieve it when needed. We input via the senses: eyes, ears, nose, mouth and touch. We process that information via the conscious mind and store the memory in the sub-conscious mind. The retrieval comes in the form of memories, thought, speech and action. However, what makes us different is that we can think and feel. A computer cannot.

The information about the little girl in the past life had been retrieved despite the fact that I did not know it was there and did not consciously access that information. I apparently stumbled across it by chance as opposed to pressing a button on a computer and deliberately extracting information.

So what button did I press to retrieve the information about the little girl? The memory was obviously in my database, but how did I access that data? What was the trigger or sequence of events that allowed me to retrieve this memory and what was it doing there in the first place? Are all our past lives stored in our memory banks? Do we have access to everything we have ever done?

There are, of course, some major differences between our minds and a computer; the main one being that we have emotions. So what part do our emotions play in what we store and retrieve from our data base? The answer to these questions was to come in so many different ways, that I came to understand both the simplicity and complexity of our mind and its storage and retrieval system.

One of the first opportunities to see the mind retrieval system at work was when 'John' came to see me after attending one of my workshops. He said he had been using meditation at home and believed he had tapped into a past life. He wanted me to help him explore this possibility a bit further. Of course, I happily agreed to do so.

John was in his thirties and had recently met a girl who interested him very much. The difference was that he had met this girl several years ago but had not pursued the friendship and lost contact with her, much to his regret. Here she was back in his life and he did not want to miss another opportunity. Successful relationships had been a problem for him and he did not want this one to be another casualty.

John also had breathing problems caused by a broken nose sustained whilst playing football. In the past life that he had tapped into, he was in love with this particular girl, but so was somebody else. The problem developed into a brawl and John, in that lifetime, sustained a broken nose as a result of the fight!

We discussed this incident and he wondered if his breathing problems originated in that lifetime and, whether he should initiate a relationship with the girl. We decided to explore the past life a bit more to see what we could find.

I guided him into a deep meditation and looked once more at the lifetime but no new information came forward. As John was obviously quite prepared to look at past lives we decided to see if there were other lifetimes that had any relevance to this issue.

We tapped into another lifetime where he found himself as a woman. She was being beaten and abused by her husband and after being thrown against the wall sustained a broken nose. This experience was not very pleasant so we moved on. I was beginning to find this repetitive pattern amusing, but kept that thought to myself.

The next lifetime found him as a male on top of a thatched roof repairing a leak. His wife was yelling at him from the ground telling him what to do. He got annoyed, lost his footing and fell off the roof. Yes, he broke his nose. By this time it was hard to contain my laughter, however, it was not over yet.

In the next lifetime, he was involved in a raiding party trying to gain entry into a castle. They were using a battering ram and guess who was at the front and ended up having his face pushed against the door? Yes, John, and he again received a broken nose.

We went through several other lifetimes each one resulting in a broken nose. Finally I decided it was time to find out whether there was a lifetime that had started this cycle of events. He went right back to pre-historic times.

He was dressed scantily in animal skins and was

out hunting food with a couple of other men, their only weapon being a type of wooden spear. They cornered a wild animal which John could not recognise, but said was about the size of a small steer. The animal charged John, pushing him over. He sustained a broken nose and the animal escaped.

By this time, John could also see the funny side of the situation and we both enjoyed a good laugh, but I was also very curious about this repetitive pattern of behaviour.

I asked John what he was feeling at that time and he expressed fear. Mind you so would I, witnessing a wild animal charging at me. However, the fear was a fear of conflict. He was a man who was supposed to be fearless in hunting or battle, but three of them had failed to capture one beast and the family would go hungry. This resulted in a loss of esteem, not only within his community, but also within himself.

He was a failure in his eyes; he had failed to provide for his family and had come back from the hunting party, not only empty handed, but also injured. Failure had been registered in the data bank as a likely outcome during times of conflict. Failure to provide for his immediate needs and failure to protect himself from injury.

When looking at the subsequent lifetimes we realised that the injury (broken nose) had been sustained during times of conflict, whether battle for survival purposes or in a relationship situation.

It was almost as if every time John was confronted with a situation that involved conflict, he would be reminded of that earlier lifetime. A time when he had sustained an injury and failed to succeed in even providing the basic necessities of life.

It would appear that when that memory was stored in the prehistoric man's memory bank, it was stored with the sense of failure. Fear that he would fail again had also been registered with that memory.

Seemingly, the difference between us and the computer is not only the emotions, but the conclusions we make based on those emotions. The computer makes conclusions based on data only; we make conclusions based on data and emotions. These conclusions are also influenced by the particular emotion and become a belief.

Had the prehistoric man conquered the beast and brought home food for his family, then the data would have been stored with positive feelings of success and self-worth. However, this was not the case and the prevailing belief was that he was a failure and unable to look out for his welfare, or those for whom he felt responsible.

Here we were today and John had already

sustained his broken nose for this lifetime during a football match. But what was interesting was that he had sustained that injury between the first and second meetings with the girl. By talking about those lives, he realised that he had not pursued the relationship the first time he met this girl, because of fear of failure. This fear was also tied into the broken nose scenario and when next in a conflict - the football match - he sustained a broken nose.

Although there were other issues involved in this cycle, this one was of most concern at the time. By looking at the repetitive behaviour patterns, John was able to see that by letting go of the fear of failure, he would be free to achieve those goals that had been eluding him for so long.

Another interesting occurrence was that before starting this session, John had extreme difficulty in breathing through his nose, but by the time he was ready to leave, he was breathing normally. He was amazed at this physiological change.

Breathing is one of the first functions affected when confronted by fear so it was appropriate that the release of that particular fear had alleviated the breathing problem. Nonetheless, it was quite a remarkable turnaround.

Recognising that the fear that had been influencing his life had its origins so long ago, enabled John to let go of the belief system that he was inadequate when it came to providing for a family, or of taking care of himself. John left determined to contact this girl from the past and let what happens happen, without fear of failure.

Helping John resolve this problem brought many answers to my questions. We obviously store our experiences or data in our memory banks with the relevant emotions attached. Taking John as an example; when confronted with similar situations, the memory bank reminded him that based on past experiences, he was likely to fail, get hurt or both. He then responded to the situation using fear and the underlying belief system of, 'I am a failure', as the main reference point and created similar situations.

Every lifetime where he repeated the behaviour pattern, that information was added to the data file in the memory bank, until the database was so large that there was no room for argument or another opinion or belief.

He had created a situation where he appeared to have no option but to continue the same behaviour pattern because it was so well entrenched. However, on reflection, one can see that in every situation he did have a choice on how to respond. Yes, he had created these situations based on previous experience but he also had free will and had the option of whether to continue the pattern or break the cycle.

In any one of those situations he could have responded differently and changed the outcome. He could have rejected the suggestion from his database that he should respond by being fearful and used a more positive attitude.

Opening up John's awareness to the repetitive pattern was one way of helping him break the cycle. Just knowing that you have done it over and over again is sometimes enough to release the fear behind that pattern of behaviour. In John's case this awareness, plus our ability to laugh at the situation, helped to break down the fear. It is not always so. Those underlying belief systems can be so stubbornly entrenched and difficult to remove that I refer to them as the hidden saboteurs. Those belief systems, which are the assumptions made by the sub-conscious mind, based on the data stored in the memory banks coupled with the emotions, trip us up when least expected. They sabotage our good intentions.

So, if emotion is one of the criteria of how we store our memories, what was the emotion that allowed me to access the information about the little girl in my past life? What belief system was operating at the time that opened up this window into the past? A past I knew nothing about consciously, yet apparently was there all the time.

As mentioned, I was practising age regression therapy techniques with a fellow student and went back to birth as part of the therapy session. What I experienced first was the little girl's indecision and some degree of fear. It occurred to me that at that time I was going through enormous change in my life and there were many decisions to be made about the new direction my life was taking.

I was studying to become a therapist and this was a complete career change for me. I would be moving out of my comfort zone into a totally new world and would be offering my services to the public. Up until this point I had been employed by others or engaged in helping my husband with his business.

Now I would be looking for people to come and see me for myself. I would be asking people to trust my knowledge and competence as a therapist. I was going through lots of doubts about my ability to be credible and acceptable, doubts that are quite normal when you are facing total change in your life.

No wonder I had tapped into the lifetime of the young girl's indecision and fear as I was experiencing the same emotions. Her indecision and fear led to her running and subsequently being caught. This left her with a sense of not knowing whether to trust her instincts again.

In this lifetime, I always wanted to be in the health care profession but postponed it until I had raised my four children, and felt determined enough to pursue my own goals. Perhaps those latent feelings of indecision and fear about trusting myself had prevented me from moving into this area much earlier in my life.

I remember meditating with my guides one day after starting on this new career direction and asking whether I was on my right path in life. I received a resounding, "Yes my child". However, something made me ask, "Did I take this new path at the right time?" and was shocked to receive the reply, "No". After asking for more information, I received, "You came into this life with three opportunities to take this path and you missed the first one and took the second". This was totally unexpected as I felt really confident that I had fulfilled my commitments to my family and was now free to do what I wanted with my life.

On further questioning about the opportunity I had missed the only response I got was, "That path no longer exists as you have taken up this path. Once you decided not to take up the first one it disappeared - it no longer exists".

I had obviously had an opportunity but had rejected it. The frustrating part was that I could not consciously remember rejecting any opportunities.

On reflection, I did have a vague memory of going through a period of having lots of ideas in my head but never following through on any of them. I would discuss them with my husband and he would encourage me to follow through, but procrastination was a popular pastime of mine at the time. It would always irk me that within a few months I would hear of somebody successfully doing exactly what I had thought about doing myself.

It occurred to me that this was probably the time I rejected the opportunity through my indecision and fear of stepping out into the unknown.

Procrastination based on fear had stopped me from moving forward. I must have decided by my inaction not to take up that path when offered.

I suddenly became grateful that I had had the courage to pick up on the second opportunity without waiting for the third. My feeling was that I would have been totally mortified if I had left my run until the third opportunity opened up. However, that is probably unfair because I gave myself those three opportunities just in case I needed them. If overcoming my own self doubts was part of my learning in this lifetime then giving myself three opportunities was the least I could do.

Making decisions was again something I was made aware of. We do make our decisions based on the information we have available at the time and dependent on our emotions. Nobody made me take up this path and nobody made me miss the first opportunity.

Have I made a mistake by missing the first one? I would not think so because I am quite happy with what I have achieved in a relatively short space of time. Had I taken up the first opportunity I may have got to this same point but at a slower pace and still be doing the same things at the same time. I will never know as once a decision is made all the other opportunities disappear and there is no way of comparing the outcome. Just as well perhaps.

Looking back I think that the belief system that had prevented me from taking up my first opportunity was still alive and well even just before I opened my holistic centre.

I moved to the city with my family and had intended starting work straight away in my new role as a therapist. I also wanted to continue my workshops that had been so popular in the country.

However, when I had settled in our new house I saw a great position advertised in the paper for an office manager with an international company. I knew I could do the job and decided to apply for the position. I was offered the job with an excellent salary package. All the right ingredients to pander to my ego and soothe my fear of moving out into my new direction.

However, within a few months I realised that I was totally unhappy doing this type of work and decided to leave despite the fact that the recession had hit and our city was one of the worst affected. Another factor was that I was having personality problems with the colleague I was working with and it was all becoming too unpleasant. I went to the Managing Director and tendered my resignation.

The response was quite unexpected. He explained that he had put me on because he felt I had the right experience and personality to set up the office and to handle the rapid growth the company had been experiencing. The present staff had been there for years but had failed to update the systems to cope with the company's new international status. He wanted somebody new who was not involved in office politics to create the necessary changes.

The MD asked me would I mind staying on long enough to put the new systems into place so that the company did not get into this position again. I agreed to stay three months to straighten out the office and find a suitable replacement so that I could then leave. He accepted my terms. He put me in charge and immediately dismissed a staff member who had been reluctant to accept the change, leaving me to carry the full workload.

I later realised that my ego had been indulged again. This and the fear of starting out on my own in the middle of a recession had certainly influenced my decision to accept the offer. I set to work to achieve my promised goal with this company so that I could leave with a clear conscience. However, during this period I questioned why I did not just leave when I resigned instead of staying on and making all this extra work for myself. I did not owe these people anything, or did I?

Since tapping into the past life of the little girl I had found that by meditating with my guides I could sometimes access a relevant past life memory. I decided to meditate on this aspect of my behaviour and seek some enlightenment about my relationship with these people.

They showed me a past life where I had been with the three directors of this company. We were generals on a battle field in the civil war in America. The four of us were formulating a battle plan but I was reluctant to support them and was indecisive through fear.

Without a unified approach we lost the battle and I had to accept responsibility for not having the courage to support them. Here was another instance where I had let my fears influence my decision making process, as they did with the little girl in the other lifetime. Suddenly, her indecisiveness seemed understandable as a history of this type of behaviour had unfolded. A bit like 'John' and his broken nose.

It all seemed to make sense of my inability to say, "No," when asked to stay on in the job. I obviously felt I owed it to them to get them through this work-place battle. It also made sense of my sudden urge to apply for the job in the first case. Nothing happens by chance. It would seem I needed to meet up with these people again to make amends for not supporting them in the past. I was certainly doing it now and making decisions was something I had to do if I wanted the job completed before my self-imposed three month deadline.

I'm pleased to say that I did achieve my goal and left on good terms. I was also more focused on where I wanted to be and what I wanted to do. My indecision was gone and I was ready to start on my new career with enthusiasm. It seemed that by rectifying my past indecisiveness, through helping those people in this lifetime, I had managed to release the fears that had been stopping me from making decisions that affected my future.

Changing the belief system by releasing the fears changes the basis on which we make our decisions. Our whole reality changes.

So there are problems
and difficulties,
be reassured if you truly
follow and trust with all
your heart,
all will be well.
All works out as it should,
just recognise this and
believe.

3

Creating Change

I was collecting the mail from my letterbox when something made me look at the group of shops across the road. An inner voice seemed to be saying that one would become vacant soon. Initially, I wondered why I was thinking that then speculated about which one it would be. I seemed to be focused on the chemist shop. With a mental shrug of the shoulders I walked back inside and thought no more about it.

I had started my practice from a really nice studio room at the back of my house. It had a great outlook and wonderful energies. It was ideal for both consultations and workshops. I had a dream of one day opening a multi-discipline practice but felt that was down the track somewhere.

Two months later a sign went up in the chemist window indicating that they were closing down. I was quite amazed as there had been no indication that they were thinking of closing. I remembered my earlier thoughts about a shop becoming vacant and wondered whether I should take the shop and start my centre. I allowed my few remaining fears to stop me from following through on the idea.

A week later, a naturopath I had met through one of my workshops rang saying she would like to work with me and asked whether I had started my centre yet. I felt I could no longer ignore all the messages I was getting and took the plunge and enquired about the shop lease.

Within a month I had taken the shop, refitted it throughout and opened the doors to the public. The centre has grown steadily from that day.

Everything happened so quickly after I let go of the fears that were creating such a blockage to my growth. I recognised that I could have said no to the naturopath and sabotaged my dream, but I didn't and having made that decision the rest just flowed.

I began to appreciate the power of negative thought not just negative thinking. Our thoughts are the products of our perception based on the data held in our sub-conscious mind. As my practice grew I became more and more aware of the power of thought.

Advertisers use visual messages through television and print media to change our belief systems. They encourage us to believe that we not only want their product but that we need it also. They change our ambivalence into desire. This example of visuals making such a difference to our belief systems made me realise that visuals or images are what are stored in the sub-conscious mind - the data in the memory bank. I reasoned that by using images we should be able to change the negative belief systems that become hidden saboteurs.

Words alone are not enough to change the belief systems; however words accompanied by images could create positive change. I was very soon able to put my theory to the test.

'Ann', a police officer, came to see me suffering from stress and emotional problems. She had recently sat for her senior constable exams and had failed for the first time in her life. All those in her squad who had undertaken this further study had passed and she felt mortified. On further investigation this was not the real issue.

A year and half earlier Ann had been raped by one of her fellow police officers, but had not reported it because of fear of ridicule and further abuse. She had to see this fellow officer quite often in the course of her duties creating extreme anxiety and consequently, her work was suffering. Ann was depressed, and felt disempowered; her self esteem was at an all time low and she had considered suicide.

I guided her into a meditative state and, using visualisation, worked with her to release some of her fears. I asked her to visualise the person who had raped her but she was too angry and frightened to look at him. This degree of fear is quite destructive and could have left her emotionally crippled. We needed to release the fear of confronting him before we could release the other emotions caught up in the rape.

This degree of fear has no form. It is just a debilitating feeling so I decided to give the fear shape and substance. Something she could see and deal with. I elected to use the visual image of kites. They can be any shape and colour and quite expressive. I asked her to describe for me; that if her fear was a kite how big would it need to be, what colour, what shape, etc. This fulfilled two objectives - it distracted her from the intense emotion of the fear and gave her something constructive to do with the fear.

I am always amazed at the creative genius of

the mind as her kite was quite spectacular. It was a huge box shape, black, almost filled the sky and the wind was pulling it in all directions. This gave us both a very clear indication of the disturbing influence of the fear and how it was affecting her life. The box shape was telling her that she was trapped within this fear - it was all around her. Filling the sky implied it was all consuming and the strong pull of the wind gave a clear message that the fear was disturbing her at the deepest level of her consciousness. While this fear existed, she was powerless to get on with her life in a meaningful way.

I asked Ann if she was willing to cut the string and let the wind take the kite away. She gladly took the opportunity to release the fear. Amusingly, she needed a chainsaw to cut the string - another indication of the power she had given the fear to control her life.

The huge sigh of relief as the string was cut was indicative of the release of this fear. We had just removed a chunk of data in the memory bank and it was quite painless and simple. I asked her once again to imagine seeing the man who raped her and she was now able to look at him and not be frightened. An enormous change in a very short time.

We went through more visual images of seeing

a cord existing between her and the man who raped her, which represented the hold she allowed him to have over her through her own fears. The cord was thick and knotted and she felt trapped. I suggested that she could cut this if she wished and give herself back her freedom. Again, she needed a chainsaw and released a huge sigh of relief when it was cut.

I invited Ann to take this opportunity to express how she felt about what he had done to her, and that she was now taking back control of her life. She realised then that she was no longer afraid of him, or angry, and that she could quite happily let him go. This liberated her, enabling her to take back her dignity and self esteem. We used some more visual images of seeing him in the street and being able to work with him without it affecting her.

At Ann's next visit the change in her was astounding. She was radiant and happy and reported that she had been able to work with him without feeling any anxiety. She was amazed that all the negative emotions had just disappeared and her feelings towards him were ambivalent. Ann could not believe the difference and was now confident about getting on with her life. She was going to sit for her exams again and was sure of passing.

We discussed some strategies to help her retain

this sense of inner peace, and spent the session helping her let go of some other fears that had come to the surface since our last meeting.

Nothing had altered except how Ann felt about past events. The rape was still a reality, but she was no longer holding onto or remembering the fear, anger and distress that this incident caused her. It was not the rape that was destroying her but the negative emotions she was holding onto. Releasing the fears allowed her to change her reality. By giving her a choice, and placing the decision making process into her consciousness, she realised she had the power to change what was happening to her. Ann exercised her free will. She could choose to stay trapped in those negative emotions or release them and set herself free.

Realising the dynamics of giving fears form and substance opened up a whole new way of working with my clients. I developed a range of different images to suit the individual needs of the client, that matched the creative genius of their sub-conscious minds. It was a journey of learning that was both challenging and exciting.

I found that by using images that were representative of the emotion or belief, then the client could recognise the influence they were having over them. Revealing what is happening on a sub-conscious level is extremely helpful when trying to create positive change. Revealing the hidden saboteurs gives you the opportunity to eliminate them.

'Ryan' brought his wife 'Suzy' to see me. She had been suffering from post-natal depression for several months and initially had become catatonic and hospitalised for a few weeks. She was on heavy medication and making very slow recovery.

Suzy had become depressed quite soon after the birth of her son and had undergone quite extensive psychiatric therapy. Her husband had to stay home with her all the time as she had become suicidal. At a time of their life when they should be looking forward to the future, they were undergoing extreme personal trauma.

I talked with her at length about her pregnancy and other events in her life. She related how she had become distressed when her husband had to be away from home for long periods during the pregnancy. He broke his leg in an accident whilst away at work and was forced to stay home towards the end of the pregnancy. She said she was glad to have him home but her anxiety actually increased after this event. It did not make sense. She was anxious when he was away, then became even more anxious when he was home convalescing.

After the birth, Suzy withdrew into herself and left the baby to her husband, too frightened to care for him and too frightened to let either of them out of her sight. She had become catatonic shortly afterwards.

Her disclosures about her life did not appear to give any reason for her obsessive fears. She had been brought up in a loving supportive family and had married a man who was equally loving and supportive. There had been no major traumas in her 25 years.

I decided to use kinesiology to find the origin of the fears. The muscle testing technique indicated that whatever belief system was behind these fears, had its beginnings in something that happened when she was six months old. Suzy remembered her mother telling her that at that age she had undergone emergency treatment for acute bronchitis. She had no conscious memory of the incident.

Regression therapy seemed to be the best tool to use so I took her back to the age of six months. Although I did not take her into deep relaxation, Suzy spontaneously deepened her state of consciousness and became the eyes and ears of the baby. Through gentle questioning the whole scene unfolded. She reported that she was having trouble breathing and that something had been put over her face. Suzy then said she felt like she was outside her body and watching the whole scene. This was said with a sense of detachment. She then calmly reported that the doctor was shouting at the nurses and repeating several times, "We're losing her. We're losing her. She's going to die". Continuing in a monotone voice, Suzy related how eventually the scene of panic subsided as the danger passed, and the medical staff felt the baby was safe. Then she made a statement that made me take notice: "Bad things happen when away from those you love". Although said in the same monotone voice, I was struck by the implication of such a belief and its ability to become a hidden saboteur.

Encouraging her to let the whole scene fade away, I brought her consciousness back to today's reality. We discussed this episode and how she felt about what she had just experienced. Suzy had never known how close to death she had come during that emergency and she was sure her parents had no idea either. Nobody had told them how serious the condition had become. We discussed how the baby had picked up on the doctor's panic and how this could have had an impact on the baby's feelings. Suzy felt that the baby was frightened because she was separated from her mother, and strange people were telling her she could die.

During my initial history taking, several minor incidents had been noted but they seemed to be totally unrelated. However, in the light of this new information they took on a whole new dimension.

When Suzy was seven she was allowed to walk home from school by herself. Being in a small country town and only a short walk to home it was considered safe. However, on one particular day some of the boys from her class were innocently teasing her, but it got out of hand and they ganged up on her and attempted to pull down her pants. She became terrified and started screaming and they ran away. Suzy raced home and insisted her mother pick her up from school thereafter.

At the age of twelve her grandmother, who lived with them, became ill and went to hospital. She died shortly after without Suzy having a chance to see her.

When she was eighteen her best friend left to get work in another town. They drifted apart as her friend had found new interests and their relationship never recovered.

Suzy married when she was twenty-two and moved to the city where her husband lived and worked. Six months later her father had a heart attack and had to retire from work and live the life of an invalid.

After Suzy became pregnant, her husband's work took him away from home and the panic attacks started. Then he had an accident at work and broke his leg.

Looking at all these events in light of the baby's fear and the belief system that was planted at that time, a pattern was emerging that made absolute sense. When she was seven and accosted by those boys she was separated from her mother, reinforcing the original belief that you are not safe when separated from those you love. Her grandmother went to hospital and never returned. More fuel for the belief system. Her best friend leaving and then losing that relationship would have taken on deeper significance because of the belief system. However, her father's heart attack after she left home would have given it greater validity.

Her husband's accident at work would have been the absolute proof to cement in the negative belief system. By the time she had her baby she would have been terrified of both caring for the child, in case she ever had to leave him and 'something awful happening to him', and equally terrified of her husband leaving her sight for the same reason. The depth of her dilemma forced her to withdraw into herself and she was unable to cope with the stress of these conflicting fears. She became catatonic.

We discussed the belief system as Suzy remembered the feelings of the baby, and it all made sense. Taking Suzy into regression and again connecting with the baby, I guided her to hold the baby in her arms. Offering a lot of love and support, and encouraging the baby to ignore what the doctor was saying, and just focus on the love and affirm that she would be all right.

Suzy then felt that the baby was feeling happier and much more comfortable. I asked her if the baby still felt frightened and Suzy replied, "No, she is safe and secure".

This visualisation changed the memory and eliminated the belief system. Neither existed any more and therefore there was no hidden saboteur. Suzy felt quite relaxed after the session and was actually smiling. Her eyes were brighter and she seemed more animated.

I saw her again three weeks later and she and her husband were both astonished and delighted with the change in Suzy's behaviour and attitude. She had taken back responsibility for her son's care, started taking an interest in her appearance again and was encouraging her husband to find a job as she felt she could now cope on her own. It was many months before she stopped all medication prescribed by the psychiatrist, however he was amazed at her rapid recovery.

With Suzy, we did not need to give the fear some sort of form like a kite, but she did need to recognise the source of her fears. Once this knowledge was brought up to the conscious mind then we were able to use the adult Suzy, to help the baby Suzy release the fear, by changing the memory. The visuals used were to re-run the film stored in the memory bank and re-write the script to achieve a happy outcome.

This experience revealed a whole new concept of not being restricted by the reality of the past. Becoming aware that we can change the memory opened up a whole new world for my fertile imagination. Wonderful new ways to match the creative genius of the mind were unfolding.

I began to realise the true nature of free will. We always have a choice and can change our reality at any time. When we are affected by some conditioning or belief from the past that is interfering with our peace of mind or well being, we can change it. What a liberating thought.

As you learn to forgive
your personality,
so do you learn
to forgive your fellow
man for seeming errors.
Train yourself then to
think in terms of love
and forgiveness in all of
your life.
Feel a most beautiful
healing take place
within you

4

The Power of Forgiveness

The credits were rolling at the end of an emotionally powerful movie when the stranger beside me leant over and sighed, "I feel as though I have just been put through the wringer". She was by herself and the movie had touched her to such a depth that she wanted to share how she was feeling. I too was feeling wrung out and welcomed the opportunity to release some of that emotion.

I really wanted to talk about how I was feeling and obviously so did she. Clearly we both felt connected, as we had rubbed shoulders whilst undergoing emotional turmoil. We exchanged sympathetic smiles and I agreed with her about it being an emotional roller-coaster ride. However, I had a friend with me and she did not and so we went our separate ways.

The movie was not real but a well-told story

evoking an emotional response, that reached deep into my subconscious. The range of emotions demanded that I make sense of how I was feeling and put it into perspective. The film had involved me in its drama and now I had to face my real world and put it behind me.

However, the unfairness, pain and heartbreak were crying out for justification. I felt like I was being asked to make a decision about who was right and who was wrong so that I could put my feelings into tidy little compartments. I talked about this film with my family and friends until it's effect on me had diminished. We discussed the way we thought the people should have behaved and how the outcome could have been different. Judgement was so easy because we needed to make sense of apparent senseless behaviour.

However, if a film about situations and people totally unknown to us can evoke that kind of judgemental response, how would we respond if we judged our own behaviour senseless or wrong? It seemed to me that we must judge ourselves guilty in the same way we judge other situations. However, what is one supposed to do with such a guilty verdict? If the depth of feeling I had about that film was any indication, then any guilty verdict I might place on myself would demand some form of punishment or retribution. I wondered how one might go about punishing oneself.

Over the years I have come across many people who have found diverse reasons and ways to inflict punishment on themselves, however one particular case really made me realise how destructive guilt can be.

'Liza' came to see me about some difficulties she was having in her life. She talked about always being there for other people but the kindness was never reciprocated. She was a quietly spoken woman in her fifties, divorced with two children. Her husband had beaten and orally abused her their whole married life. He was an alcoholic and gambler who often left her with no money for food or other essentials. When she finally left him, her two sons abused her for abandoning them and their father. Her sons by this time were in their early twenties and had left home so their attitude was hard to fathom.

She felt she had always given to them and, now they were adults, they did not need her as much and it would be all right to have a life of her own. Instead, they made demands upon her time and generosity citing her abandonment as grounds for their requests. She still gave in to them even if it meant going hungry herself.

Her sense of self worth was at an all time low and she was considering suicide as a last resort. The only thing stopping her was that she believed it was a sin to kill herself and that there must be others who were worse off than herself.

Liza came to me to find some strength to get on with her life and see if there was any negativity stopping her getting a job. She had been unemployed for nine months and was getting quite concerned.

This was a woman who felt completely alone and friendless in the world. Even her mother abused her and told her she was a failure and should go back to her husband. The one phrase she used over and again to explain why people treated her in such a way was, "I am bad".

I asked her why she thought she was bad but she could not answer except to reflect that everybody kept telling her so. I had a strong feeling that this woman was just going through life on remote control. She was walking around and speaking but the essential part of her was not there. She seemed disconnected from her inner self. I wondered what hurt had made this woman retreat to this degree. Yes, her life had been full of abuse but she seemed to take it all in her stride as if she deserved it in some way.

We spent the first session changing the obvious belief system of low self worth, using kites and other images, to help release the control she had allowed other people to have over her. One of my favourites for this type of attitude is for the client to see herself as a puppet and cut the strings, thereby restoring control over herself. The release she felt was reflected in the profusion of tears that were streaming down her face. I always feel such joy when watching such positive change and liberation in others.

However, her next statement stunned me. She sobbed, "This is the first time I have cried since I was nine". Here was a woman in her fifties who had experienced enormous hurt and trauma in her life and she had not be able to cry since she was a child. What on earth had happened to her when she was nine to lock away her emotions to such a degree?

Unfortunately, the answer to this question would have to wait for the next session as I felt she had experienced enough for one day, and would need time to assimilate the changes we had created before exploring the nine year old.

The change in Liza at the next session was amazing. With such pride she told me that she had informed one of her sons that he would have to pay for his speeding fine as she had no money to spare. She was quite animated as she explained, "I listened to his abusive language and threats without getting angry and I repeated that I would not be able to help him this time". The delight and joy she experienced by being able to say, "No", was just wonderful to behold. However, her next statement was even more revealing about the depth of change she had undergone. She laughed, "He got very angry when I did not give in to his abusive language. I think he was quite confused". I expect he was. He had never heard his mother say, "No", before. He had always been able to manipulate her just like a puppet.

Liza had improved enormously, but she still had this deep need to do things for everybody else and neglect her own welfare. Also, she was still unable to obtain employment. Her belief in herself still had a long way to go.

I decided it was time to explore the nine year old. I asked Liza about her childhood and she said she had scant memory of when she was young, but remembered her mother locking her in the cupboard under the stairs as punishment. I asked her about those experiences and how it felt being locked away.

She talked about being bad when she was young and how she was always being punished. She hated being locked in the cupboard but accepted it as part of her lot in life. She recalled quite calmly that there were mice and nasty crawling things in there, but reflected that if she thought about being somewhere else she could cope. I had this very clear image of the child shifting her consciousness by pretending to be somewhere else, and therefore losing touch with her reality. Her way of coping was to retreat into her imagination.

I discussed with her the need to find out what happened when she was nine that stopped her from being able to cry. She could not remember, so I took her into a state of deep relaxation to explore this period of her life.

Liza instantly recalled being in the cupboard and the horror of these experiences came back to her. She felt most uncomfortable and wanted to imagine being somewhere else. She had become the nine year old. I asked her why she was in the cupboard and her reply was the now familiar, "Because I am bad". I asked her what she had done that had been judged to be bad. "I never do as I am told", was her mournful response.

Liza had been locked in the cupboard every time she had been disobedient. No wonder she had allowed her husband and children to dominate her life. She was terrified of being disobedient and therefore being punished. The result was that she had allowed the people in her life to control her.

This made sense of her behaviour, but we still did not know what had happened to the nine year old, who had retreated within herself to the point where she was unable to cry. I asked her to tell me why she was in the cupboard and an incredible story unfolded.

Liza was a child who did not make friends easily and found it difficult to handle the normal schoolyard teasing and bullying. She befriended another student, Julie, who was extremely sickly and was also treated badly by the other students. They found solace in one another because of their own insecurities. Julie suffered from asthma and often had severe attacks necessitating absences from school. This left Liza alone and she worried about her friend when she was away, longing for her return.

Julie lived about eight kms away and therefore it was difficult for them to visit each other unless they used public transport, but money was always short in both households.

At the time in question, Julie had been sick for a few days and Liza was worried about her and desperately wanted to see her. In her mind she believed that if she could see her friend then she could help her get better. A belief influenced by Liza's deep need to have her friend back at school with her so she would no longer be alone. Liza pestered her mother for the money to visit her friend. Her mother refused and Liza became quite agitated resulting in her being placed in the cupboard as punishment.

This incarceration lasted for the whole week-end with Liza also receiving beatings to her legs because she was continually crying. She was released from this prison on Monday to go to school, but by this time her legs were swollen and she had difficulty in walking. On arrival she found her friend was still absent. Her anxiety was such that she immediately left school, deciding to walk to Julie's house despite the distance and her painful legs.

It was early afternoon when she arrived, exhausted but pleased with herself that she had made it. Her excited knock on the door was answered by Julie's grandmother. Liza asked to see her friend only to be told, "Julie died two days ago. Go away, we don't need you here".

To say that she was devastated would be to totally understate her feelings on hearing these words. Her whole world fell apart. She had lost her only friend and she felt responsible. Her one thought was that if she could have managed to see Julie earlier, then her friend would not have died. Liza felt responsible for Julie's death because she was not there. Had she not been bad, then she would not have been locked up for those days and she could have saved Julie.

Her thoughts were of course totally irrational.

There was nothing the nine year old Liza could have done to change the outcome. Julie had had a severe asthma attack and died. Her family were distraught and had no thoughts for Liza whom they hardly knew. Liza was left to walk home again completely consumed by guilt and despair. She never cried again. The pain of her guilt forced her to retreat into herself and emotionally she placed herself back in the cupboard. She now truly believed she was bad and needed to be punished.

However, I now understood her deep need to help others. She was acting out what she really wanted to do for her friend. Her guilt was that she had let her friend down by being bad. She needed to punish herself but also make up for not being there for her friend by being there for everybody else. Her whole life from that moment on was one of self-punishment and a fixation on helping others. A complete entrapment of her own making.

I had listened to this story as it unfolded, only commenting when I felt Liza needed direction or encouragement to go on. I now had to help her understand that she was not to blame. We had to change the belief system that declared, "I am bad, I deserve to be punished".

I asked Liza to visualise seeing herself in the cupboard and encouraged her to give the nine year old a hug and let her know how much she was loved. Again the profusion of tears as she allowed herself to feel loved. All she had ever wanted was to be loved, and Julie was the only one she felt ever loved her for herself. Now she was being given the opportunity to love the nine year old, and therefore giving love to herself.

Before we can love anybody else we must first learn to love and respect ourselves. Not a love based on ego and pride, but a love that liberates us to take responsibility for our own well-being without judgement. This was the love that Liza was allowing herself to experience - unconditional love.

I asked today's Liza to take nine year old Liza by the hand and I took her through each step of those three days, helping her to see that it was not her fault and she was not bad. We changed the memory and eventually Liza was able to accept that she was not to blame and able to forgive herself. I then asked Liza to accept the child back, to imagine merging herself with the child so that there was just one of them, the Liza of today.

Then, the most incredible thing happened. Liza still had her eyes closed and focused on accepting the child back but as the transformation took place she started touching herself all over exclaiming, "My goodness, I have breasts. My legs are so big. I know I have children but I don't know how I did that." She had emotionally spent the last forty years being the nine year old stuck in the cupboard whilst the physical part of her had gone through all the motions of growing up and having a family. It was the most incredible sight. We were both laughing and crying over the magnitude of leaping forty years in a few minutes.

In time, I restored her to full consciousness and with her eyes wide open she again exclaimed at the size of her hands, staring at them intently both intrigued and dismayed at the result of years of wear and tear. Then the legs and all those other body parts that looked unusual to her nine year old eyes came under scrutiny. It was an extremely moving moment for both of us and full of wonderment. It was like she had just woken up after a forty year sleep and was seeing her world with new eyes.

We discussed what had happened to her and realised that, because of her guilt, she had condemned herself to be locked in the cupboard, until she had been sufficiently punished for the crime of being bad. Unfortunately, being both judge and jury, she had never known how to terminate the punishment for a crime she considered unforgivable. The crime of being bad and letting down her friend.

Liza had great difficulty in understanding how she could do this to herself, but realised that nobody could have done it but herself. We then had an intense discussion about not feeling guilty about punishing herself. She started to laugh saying, "It's just like me to start the whole process over again. No, I fully forgive myself, and I am going to get on with what is left of my life".

She left the session literally a new woman ready to be her own person. She talked about what she really wanted to do and was starting to make plans before she left. I was fully aware of the almost magical transformation I had been privileged to be part of and witness. It also added to my understanding of our ability to inflict enormous punishment on ourselves when we decide we are guilty.

Liza was able to stop judging herself and therefore stop the punishment she had been inviting into her life. She had taken back control, and by releasing the nine year old had become centred and focused in the here and now. She was no longer working from the locked cupboard, she was making decisions based on today's reality. She had taken back her personal power, the power to be herself. Self empowerment.

Liza was amazed to report at our next session that people were behaving differently towards her and her family did not seem to be so aggressive or frightening. She found that she could say no to others when it was in her best interest to do so. She also reported that she was now eating well and looking after herself. Even more amazing for her was that a male friend had asked her out for dinner and she had accepted. Something she had shied away from previously.

Her whole world had changed because she had changed. She was no longer seeking punishment, so those around her ceased to give her the punishment she sought. Changing the belief system changed the reality.

I started to think that it would be much easier if there was someone up there judging us, then at least the punishment would be realistic and presumably have a designated beginning and end. However, we have free will and we make all the decisions in our life. We are totally responsible for what so called punishment we bring into our lives. We are also totally responsible for ending the punishment by forgiving ourselves.

You know, life would be much simpler and easier if we did not judge ourselves, in fact, if we did not judge at all. Accepting ourselves as we are would open us up to so much more learning and positive experiences. It would also help us to accept others and their right to be where they are at any given moment.

I really think one of the hardest things we are

asked to do is to accept another person's right to be who they are, without judgement. However, if we were able to do so, it would create such contentment that life would be a joyful experience.

The choice is always ours. We can judge ourselves or others to be guilty and set up a pattern of punishment, or we can choose to see our behaviour as part of the learning process and let it go. We always have a choice, but what if the origin of the judgement was not in this lifetime?

'Katie' came to see me after attending one of my workshops. I had only seen her wearing dark clothing and her whole demeanour was one of sadness and despair. She wore little make-up and had a general air of careless attention to her appearance. Her participation in the workshop was limited to asking questions that reflected her sadness and sense of powerlessness. I was pleased she had made an appointment to see me privately as I knew she needed help.

Her opening comments were dramatic, "Something awful is going to happen to my children, and I don't know how to prevent it". I encouraged her to talk about this fear and what basis she had for it. A history of paranoid behaviour based on suspicion and distrust followed with Katie being hospitalised for psychiatric care on two occasions. She was presently on anti-depressant medication.

She explained that she firmly believed that either her husband was going to kill their son, or their son would kill his sister. She also believed her husband would eventually harm her. She was frightened of him and only stayed with him to protect her son from being murdered. The belief that these events were just a matter of time was the cause of her anxiety. Her children had left home and her son was living overseas. He was too far away for her, "to keep an eye on", and this exacerbated her anxiety. She wanted to learn how to relieve her anxiety and save her children.

On questioning her in more detail there did not seem to be any reason for her fears based on this lifetime's experiences. I decided to investigate her past lives.

In the first lifetime I was given, she was the mother of twins and they had drowned. She felt totally responsible for their deaths even though I could see that she could not have prevented the drownings. I explained this to her but her response was, "I must have been responsible". I decided to look at other lifetimes to see if I could find the origin of this belief that she is responsible for the behaviour of other people.

I went back many years to when she was the chaperone to a young woman of wealth. Her father had arranged a marriage for financial reasons, but she was already emotionally committed to somebody else. Katie secretly sympathised with her young charge and turned a blind eye when the secret lovers ran away. The father pursued them and killed them both, the boy for his insolence and his daughter for the disgrace she brought upon his house.

Katie was blamed for not controlling her charge, and because of the outcome, took responsibility for the two deaths. She judged herself to be totally to blame and killed herself.

So, after this lifetime we are left with a father who took the life of his daughter and her lover as a result of his ego and rage. A daughter and her lover going to their deaths believing that love has it's price, and the chaperone taking all the blame and going to her death believing she is guilty.

All of these players had strong unresolved conflicts to work through and release. Because most of them terminated that lifetime shortly after the event, then it was almost inevitable that they would need to come together in another lifetime to resolve these issues.

I was able to see a series of lifetimes where the father, daughter, lover and chaperone had been re-incarnating over and over again and in each instance somebody ended up dying either prematurely or violently. It was as if they were caught up in a tit for tat pattern of behaviour. I'll kill you this time and you kill me the next, and occasionally varying the formula by dying 'accidentally'. In every scenario Katie took the blame, by assuming she should have been able to do something to stop them hurting themselves.

Today she was sub-consciously waiting for the inevitable death to occur, not sure whose turn it was to 'do the deed'. No wonder she was displaying symptoms of paranoia. No wonder she was depressed, sad and full of despair.

I explained to her that she needed to forgive the chaperone, as she had taken responsibility for somebody else's behaviour. We can never be responsible for anything but our own actions as everybody has free will. The father through his own rage had placed the blame on Katie and she had accepted it. Once accepted it became part of her reality and she became responsible for their subsequent behaviour.

They all became trapped in a cycle of behaviour that was based on blame, guilt, fear and rage. They were all victims of their emotions trapped in the past, playing out the scene over and over again. The settings changed and the names of the players were different, but the actions were the same. We needed to release the chaperone of the blame and hand back responsibility for the deaths to the father. If they wanted to continue playing this game of tit for tat then that was their responsibility, however I wanted Katie to relinquish her part and move on.

She was caught up in a never ending cycle of punishment and retribution, of which she had no part to play except to take responsibility for the outcome. She could not win and was caught in a trap of her own making.

I took Katie into deep relaxation and my first task was to release her from the repetitive behaviour pattern she had created, and asked her to see herself on a round wooden treadmill like a mouse might have in its cage. She was horrified to see herself exhausted, old and full of despair. I encouraged her to help that part of herself off the treadmill and liberate herself from the repetitive behaviour pattern. This part of herself needed encouragement and strengthening and I used other visual images to help restore full vitality.

We then burnt the treadmill giving the subconscious mind a clear message that this behaviour was now finished. The relief at being able to let go of the destructive behaviour pattern was immense. Katie felt encouraged and more at peace.

I then asked her to visualise seeing the chaperone. She became quite emotional explaining that she looked so sad. Katie could tell me exactly what she looked like and all the conflicting emotions she was experiencing. She had allowed herself to see the chaperone at the point where she was considering suicide.

I suggested Katie give her a hug and let her know that she did not blame her any more and that there is another way of thinking and feeling. Encouraged, we took the chaperone through the events again and helped her to see that there was nothing she could have done to change the events. The daughter decided the outcome when she disobeyed her father. The choice was hers and the issue was between her and her father.

As the chaperone, she was the innocent bystander. The father sought to release his anger and presumably guilt by placing the blame on her. She had a choice of whether to accept or reject. We gave the chaperone that choice again and with encouragement she decided to reject the blame, handing it back to the father.

Katie's emotional release was proof that the belief system had been changed. I asked her to imagine a cord between herself and the chaperone, and to cut it indicating that she had severed this past connection. She then hugged the chaperone and released her to the light.

After using some other images to improve her

self esteem and well being, I brought her back to full consciousness and discussed what we had done. Katie expressed a strange feeling of lightness and inner calmness. Strange, because she could not remember ever feeling so peaceful, and hoped it would last. I explained that the changes she had created today would last because they had been done on such a deep level.

She came to see me a month later and was wearing a bright yellow top and white slacks, a big smile, a new hairstyle and make-up. I mentioned her changed image and she said, "I can no longer abide wearing those dowdy clothes". She related how she had undergone a total change of attitude. She no longer feared her family destroying themselves and had stopped worrying about them. She had started looking after herself and eating foods that were more nutritious.

Her husband had initially become confused about her total change of behaviour and threatened to have her put back in hospital. She decided to leave him, as her reason for staying with him no longer existed and she was now making plans to undertake further study to improve her mind. The change in her was nothing short of incredible. I rejoiced in her liberation.

Having released herself from that belief system she no longer had to be part of their on-going saga, so it was appropriate for her to leave. It is quite possible that once she handed back responsibility for the deaths to the father, then it would give him a chance to release the negative emotions he was caught up in. On enquiring about his behaviour, she reported that once he knew she meant what she said and he recognised that she was completely in control of her life, he changed his attitude towards her. Maybe this was the beginning of him being able to resolve his emotional impasse. Perhaps the children as well.

The father judged the chaperone to be guilty. The chaperone accepted the guilty verdict and proceeded to make amends by being there for them in every subsequent lifetime. She had stopped herself from moving on and growing. She had become bogged down in self blame and remorse, but she was powerless to stop their behaviour as she had no control over their actions.

When we seek to judge or be judged we hand over our power to our emotions and other people. Self punishment is soul destroying behaviour but we do have choices and we can stop this destructive behaviour at any time.

Now is as good a time as any other. It's your choice.

Forgive as you wish to be
forgiven,
these words come to your
with love.
When your emotions
threaten
to overwhelm you
just forgive and all will be
forgiven and
you will be blest with love.

5

The Power of Choice

It was Saturday morning and the house was stirring to a new day. Harry, our very spoilt Cavalier King Charles spaniel, was yawning and thinking of getting out of his basket. The bedroom doors to my adult children's rooms were resolutely shut indicative of a late Friday night. They will get up when they are ready, no need to rush. The birds were chirping and a gentle breeze was wafting through the flywire door.

I sat down with my cup of tea to read the Saturday newspapers at my leisure. An absolute luxury after the discipline of week days. Saturday's papers are so big you can spend all day just browsing through all the journalistic offerings.

I don't deliberately set out to read the gloom and doom but sometimes it is difficult to avoid stories that are designed to stir the passions. The writers appear to deliberately slant the stories to highlight the tragedy or injustice of a particular situation.

On this particular day there were two stories that caught my attention. The first one was about a twelve year old girl who had received a bone marrow transplant after years of suffering from leukaemia. Her parents described her recovery as nothing short of a miracle. Joy had been restored to the household. However, the thrust of the story was not about celebrating her survival but of highlighting the tragedy that she had been killed in a traffic accident the day before.

Now, you may think I am strange, but I could not help laughing. This child had obviously made a decision to leave and all the medical technology in the world was not going to stop her going when the time was right. I was, of course, mindful of the feelings of the parents but it was like I could sense the big picture and recognise that she was doing what she wanted to do with her life. Not on a conscious level of course, but on a deep subconscious level. It was obviously what she had planned for herself.

With a light chuckle I continued reading and found another story that made me again think about the choices we make. This time it was of a man who had been receiving treatment for a life threatening condition and part of the treatment was a blood transfusion. The condition was no longer an issue but he got "AIDS" from the blood he received. I could almost hear him saying, "Well, try and fix that one".

By this time I was really laughing at the irony of the circumstances. Luckily, nobody was around to ask what was so amusing. I may have had difficulty in explaining it to their satisfaction.

I thought about the little girl and wondered what would have happened had the leukaemia been allowed to take its course. Would the parents have come to terms with the child's illness and prepared themselves for her death? Would they have come to that point where each could say good-bye and feel satisfied that they had said to each other all that needed to be expressed? Would the death have been a sorrowful but spiritually fulfilling event?

We will never know because the child was killed suddenly and nobody had a chance to say good-bye. Maybe that was the only way the child could go, without the pressure from the parents to stay. To judge this as a tragedy is to intimate that we have no control over our lives and some external force has interfered with our plans and our future.

However, if we have free will and we choose what happens in our life, then the decision to go must have been her own. Anything else does not make sense. I would like to think that the parents have moved on and have been able to learn from their daughter, not holding onto her memory and becoming victims of the past.

However, our man with AIDS was a different matter. He had undergone therapy to cure a condition and was left with another, that at this juncture is incurable. It is almost as if he wants to suffer in some way and wants to make sure that he cannot be cured. If we invite punishment into our lives then this man is making sure that his punishment lasts until his death. Hopefully, that will be the end of it and he can get on with the next stage of his spiritual growth. Either way he chooses his life and his death.

I had this choice shown to me in a very distinct way. My uncle, whom I loved dearly, decided that there was no afterlife and when you are dead, you are dead. End of story. We had many a discussion on our differences of opinion, even to the point of entering into an agreement that when he was gone he would come back and tell me whether I was right. We even laughingly shook hands on the deal. He was that kind of man and we had that kind of relationship. Open and friendly.

In retirement, he became an active member of the local bowling club, playing up to three times a week. His Irish background came to the fore when there was company, wine and good conversation. He also loved B grade cowboy movies, was the typical male chauvinist and disliked being restricted in any way. He was always the life of the party, told wonderful jokes and loved being the centre of attention.

One day, he just dropped dead on the bowling green after playing for a full day. He had enjoyed afternoon tea with his wife and other members and went out to finish the game. He picked up his bowl and just dropped where he stood from a heart attack. We were all shocked at the suddenness of his death and dismayed that we had not had a chance to say good-bye.

However, on reflection, I remembered my uncle laughingly telling everybody over and over again, "I want to go before my wife, I want to go with my boots on like the cowboys, and I don't want a lingering death, it has to be quick". Well, if one could put in an order I think he did a pretty good job.

I realised that he had verbalised his request so often that he had made it a reality. Either that, or he knew how he had planned to go and was just letting everybody know so that they would not be surprised when it happened. Either way it does not really matter, but it did make me think, and also have a laugh at the way he departed. He always was one for wanting his own way. He spent most of his working life giving orders to others so he was used to organising and having things work out the way he planned. Well done uncle, an exit successfully orchestrated and accomplished.

I went with the rest of my family to view him in his coffin as our only opportunity to say good-bye. It seemed strange not hearing his laugh and seeing his wonderful smile. He was certainly not there in that wooden box. For some strange reason the funeral director had placed plastic flowers in his clasped hands, obviously unaware that my uncle is neither a gardener nor in the habit of holding flowers. My amusement at this incongruous sight was interrupted by a strong voice in my head demanding, "Take those prissy things out of my hands".

I looked around to see if the others had heard, but they were deep in their own thoughts. I looked at the flowers again and heard the words repeated in the same authoritative tone he used to direct people whilst alive. I gently removed them whilst the others weren't looking and was rewarded for my efforts with a quiet, "Thank you".

Our conversation did not go beyond those few words, but I sensed that this was his way of letting me know that he was still around and in control of his thoughts. Incidentally, my watch stopped for twenty minutes whilst we were in there, something it had never done before or since. If he was responsible it would be his style to make me take notice and to keep us there a little bit longer. Arranging our lives to the last moment but true to his word, he had kept his part of our handshake agreement. I knew he was all right so was able to say good-bye with peace of mind.

If we choose our life and our death, then presumably we choose whom we decide to share our life with, our gender and our place in the family. After all, it is the dynamics of our position in the family that can influence our perspective and sometimes our behaviour. Certainly our learning. This cannot be a chance or random option, we must have chosen our time of birth in the same way we choose our death.

Alice came to see me about relationship problems with her sister. She was the eldest of three girls and was devoted to her parents and sisters. However, Alice was always in conflict with her youngest sister, Merle. This was now causing some distress as her father had recently died having survived his wife by only two years and the estate had to be settled.

Alice related a long history of antagonism from her sister starting almost from the moment Merle could talk. Alice felt that her sister hated or resented her for some reason which seemed to have no grounds. She was loath to confront her as any communication seemed to end in angry words.

Being the eldest, Alice felt she should handle their parents' affairs but Merle had taken over that role when their mother died. She had taken their father into her own house and had sold up the family home keeping only those keepsakes she had room to accommodate. Alice had difficulty in contacting her father by phone because Merle would screen the calls. When Alice had visited her father, Merle was always nearby listening to their conversation.

Alice wanted to be involved in the funeral arrangements but her sister had it all arranged before she notified her of his death. Merle had assumed the role of the eldest child displacing Alice. Alice had offered to help settle the estate but was told by Merle that it was all under control. She felt disconnected from her father and was now concerned that the particular keepsakes he had promised her would not be honoured by her sister. Of even greater concern however, was that the family would fall apart now that their common link was gone.

Alice wanted help to understand her sister's attitude and to be able to attend the funeral without it becoming uncomfortable and disagreeable. She was at a loss to know how to deal with her sister and this was causing a lot of heartache. Alice felt strongly that if she did not resolve the issue now there would never be another opportunity.

I decided to see if there was a past life that could explain her sister's behaviour and obvious antagonism towards Alice. As I closed my eyes to focus, my thoughts were interrupted by the impression that Alice's mother had lost a child and on asking the question received an affirmative. Apparently her mother had twins, a boy and girl, before Alice was born, both of whom died shortly after birth. The mother was quite grief stricken and did not talk about them very much, focusing all her love and attention on the three subsequent children she bore. Alice knew nothing about the circumstances of their birth or death and consequently felt there was some mystery about it.

I could sense the mother's grief at the time of

their death, however the twin's energies were more confusing. I sensed that there was something unresolved about their choice to be born, almost as if they were coming to do something together but could not come to an agreement about the logistics. Because the life purpose was not clearly resolved and decided upon, they left as soon as they arrived. It was interesting for me to experience this inner conflict of purpose, because in the past I had only looked at people who had survived, not those who had left so early.

They had chosen birth, but there were unresolved issues between them, so they decided to terminate the lifetime because they could not agree on their basic life purpose. That may seem a bit harsh for the mother after going through all that hard work, but it may well be that part of her life's purpose may have been to experience that grief.

However, the really interesting fact I discovered was that Alice was the female twin who came back at the next opportunity. The male twin was her sister Merle. Assuming that being first born was one of the experiences they both wanted included in this lifetime then Alice came back in the right position for herself. However, if being male and first born was part of Merle's criteria then she would have been most uncomfortable being the youngest and a female.

I discussed this premise with Alice and she felt it made sense. She explained that Merle had always been the dominant one in the family and had strong masculine qualities. She also had great difficulty in expressing or sharing emotions. She said Merle's behaviour was very much that of being jealous of Alice's first born position in the family. She had spent her whole life endeavouring to assume the role of eldest in the family by trying to wrest it from her sister Alice. The middle sister did not seem to be involved in this scenario and had managed to remain friends with both her siblings.

Alice recalled many instances throughout their childhood and subsequent adulthood where her sister's behaviour reflected this frustration with her younger sister status. It all made a lot of sense.

I wanted to explore why Merle had not come in as the eldest when the opportunity presented itself. What I received indicated that Merle wanted to be male, but the next child was female; and the next. I reasoned that she must have wanted to be in this particular family so decided to come as a female rather than not come at all. It appeared that Alice was someone with whom she needed to resolve some issues.

I was now curious as to why they had initially intended to come in as equals and what issues they needed to resolve. So again I looked for a past life to explain their conflict.

They had been brothers in an African tribe, Merle being the younger. Alice had been favoured by his father and given all the privileges of the elder son including sacred information handed down through the generations. Merle, as the younger son, had felt unimportant and neglected.

When it came to making family decisions the elder son was always consulted and in the due course of time when the father died, he assumed the role of head of the family. Merle, as the younger son, had never had the opportunity to contribute and felt disempowered. Jealousy ran rife within him and left him frustrated and unfulfilled.

In this lifetime he wanted to come as the male and eventually become the head of the household, but the unresolved jealousy resulted in the conflict that terminated the first chance at life. Needing to prove to Alice that she was just as capable of making the family decisions, she eventually came into this life as the youngest child determined to take over the role of head of the family.

She had spent her life doing just that. However, she was still not happy as the jealousy that was the motive behind her behaviour was still active. Somehow we needed to let her know that she had nothing to prove to Alice and that the past could be released.

Guiding Alice in relaxation therapy, I asked her to visualise seeing Merle in a place that represented neutral ground. A place that was new and did not belong to either of them: sitting under a tree on a pleasant hilltop.

Alice's immediate response was that her sister was angry and did not want to communicate, however with persistence we were able to open up dialogue. Alice found that by talking to Merle in this subconscious way they were both able to express their feelings. Alice 'heard' all Merle's complaints and recognised her feelings of low self worth.

Through her thoughts she explained to Merle that all she ever wanted was to be friends and understand her. If looking after their parents was helping her to feel better about herself then that was all right. Alice explained that she did not want to be excluded completely, however, Merle retorted that that was just how she had felt in the past. Alice expressed that she had never intended to exclude her and hoped that they could become closer in the future. The impression Alice had from Merle was that she would think about it.

I decided to work with the African brothers. I asked Alice to visualise seeing these two and asked how she felt when looking at them. She felt sad. I asked her to visualise talking to them and getting the elder brother to talk to the younger brother and involve him more in the decision making process. We set about changing the memory of the past life as far as Alice was concerned and therefore changing the negative emotions and beliefs that still existed in that lifetime. At the end it felt better and the brothers were friends.

I returned Alice's focus to talking to Merle under the tree and she said Merle had decided to be friends. She no longer wanted to punish Alice for being the first born and was willing to work with her in the interest of family harmony. Alice was delighted with this change of attitude and hugged her as a thank you.

On returning Alice to full consciousness we discussed what we had done and some strategies for handling the day of the funeral. She felt more confident at the conclusion of the session.

At our next visit Alice was delighted to report that Merle had been most conciliatory at the funeral and had even suggested that they should keep in touch. A complete turn about in attitude and behaviour. Alice decided to let Merle take the initiative and not be disappointed if she did not call. She felt Merle needed some space to allow whatever changes had been made to have time to become reality.

After a few months Alice was able to report a

comfortable relationship even if it was not as close as she would wish. She was able to accept Merle's decision **and re**spect her space.

These two sisters had deliberately chosen to come into the same family to resolve their differences. I had a very clear impression by this time that Alice had agreed to help Merle release her jealousy and find peace. Maybe in another lifetime they can become closer, or maybe it is not necessary for them to have any further interaction. Hopefully, whatever had been interfering with their inner peace was now over and they can enjoy whatever other learning they have also chosen to include in this lifetime.

So, if we choose which family we want to join, then it would stand to reason that we would also choose race, culture, religion or even geographic location. For if we make the decisions as to what lessons we are going to learn, then we would pick the people who can give us the best opportunity to learn.

That includes whatever conditioning the parents can give us, and what our relationship is with our siblings and other family members. Also, what culture best suits our needs; whether we need to be exposed to any particular philosophy or religion and what kind of people we need in our lives to help us resolve our issues. Each of these ingredients gives us a broad scope to create the exact environment that is right for us.

We may choose to be born in a country where poverty is rife, to enable us to learn the lessons of self-acceptance. Or, where life is subject to restriction, whether that be political, religious or economic, to learn inner strength. Maybe in a past life we had been intolerant and we want to learn tolerance, so we may choose to be born into a culture that demands acceptance.

Whatever scenario you have created in your life this time, allow yourself to recognise the lessons you have chosen. They will always be positive lessons, not negative. If you have been judgemental in the past, then acceptance will be your lesson. If you have been fearful, then love is what you would have chosen. If you have been hurt then forgiveness will be your major lesson. You will recognise your lesson if you know what negative emotions are always coming to the fore. They are there to remind you that these are what you are endeavouring to overcome.

The family you have chosen are there to help you learn these lessons, particularly those people with whom you always seem to be at odds. They are probably reflecting back to you the lessons you have chosen.

Tess asked me to help her with her food

allergies. She had reached the stage where she was extremely limited in what she could eat. If we choose everything that happens to us then she had chosen these allergies. There had to be an underlying cause and in my experience people who create allergies usually have rejected themselves on some level. Any form of rejection is a judgement that states something is not worthwhile. If we reject ourselves, then the judgement is against ourselves and we decide we are not worthwhile. Sometimes this judgement can become as severe as self hatred.

Discussing this philosophy with Tess revealed that she despised her husband because he tried to dominate her. She talked about him making all the decisions and treating her and the children with disdain during their married life. I asked her why she stayed with a man that treated her in this way and her response was, "I would leave him if I could afford to leave. I have no means of support".

Tess and her husband were quite comfortable and if she left the marriage there would be a settlement that would allow her to live with some degree of ease. She also had adult children who were settled and would be prepared to assist her in the short term. Her perception that she could not afford to leave had no basis in fact, so there had to be another reason for her to feel so trapped. We decided to investigate further.

We took her back to birth and found that her feelings of low self worth were evident even then, reporting that the baby was feeling nervous about its new life. She also had a sense of knowing what lessons she needed to learn and who she had chosen to help her. Imagine her surprise when she found that her husband was one of the people she had asked to help her in this lifetime. They had spent several lifetimes together and understood each other. You see her major lesson for this lifetime was to learn independence, to learn to make her own decisions and stand on her own two feet.

All during their marriage her husband had been doing his best to goad her into retaliating and taking control of her life. He was making all the decisions, and she let him do it, while his actions and words were designed to force her into taking a stand. The more dominating he became the more she retreated. We discussed his behaviour in this new light and she could see that it could be interpreted in that way, so we decided to release her feelings of low self worth.

She felt trapped in the marriage so I used the image of being trapped in a cage. Again the subconscious mind gave us a clear image of how trapped she felt. She was locked inside a cage that was so small that she could neither stand up or lay out straight. She could only crouch down without moving. This was how restricted and disempowered she was feeling, no wonder she could not stand up for herself. It was not necessary to find the origin of this belief as the image was graphic enough to convince Tess of its validity. She desperately wanted to be released from this uncomfortable position.

I simply suggested that she reach into her pocket and find the key to open the door. It never ceases to amaze me how this simple suggestion will create the desired effect. By giving people back the power to release themselves they immediately feel stronger. Once liberated from the cage they feel a huge release of emotion and a shift in perception. They are no longer trapped.

Tess' response was quite emotional, and though predictable, was no less exciting. It was then easy to get Tess to forgive her husband and accept his help. It was also important for her to forgive herself for becoming trapped and disempowered. I then conveyed some other images that gave the subconscious mind the new perception that Tess was back in charge of her life, plus some other suggestions to raise her self esteem. She left our session with a completely different outlook on life.

At our next session Tess reported that her husband appeared to be more mellow and less authoritarian in his behaviour towards her and she was feeling much better about herself. She was able to eat the foods that previously had caused allergies and announced that she had decided to stay in the marriage. "He is so pleasant now that we are getting on really well, there is no reason to leave", she told me with delight.

Obviously these two can complete this lifetime in harmony, having concluded what they came to achieve. He will have his own lessons apart from helping Tess, and she will have other minor issues to resolve, but the major lesson is out of the way.

As I tell my students; when we come into a lifetime we write the script, are the producer and director of the production, and of course, take star billing. We choose our supporting actors and other bit players. We also agree to be supporting actors and bit players in other people's productions. When we arrive we have all the details in place and are ready to start the performance. However, because we have free will, we also have the option to re-write the script at any time. So, although everything is pre-arranged, nothing is pre-determined. If we re-write the script then we change the outcome.

We are always in control of our lives, but once we come into a physical existence we lose sight of the original plot, and go about re-writing the script to fit what we believe to be the truth of the matter.

A belief that is continually changing depending on what data is in the subconscious mind. Data that is continually being added to every day, depending on our responses and experiences. No wonder we lose the plot now and again, especially if we have re-written the script to the point where the storyline is going nowhere.

Then, we have the choice as to whether to stay or go. It's our decision, our choice, our script, our outcome.

To find the centre of truth, go within, for all knowledge dwells within the centre of your heart. The way to truth is to be in contact with the spirit.

6

The Big Picture

My son lives in a remote area of the Northern Territory and on a recent visit I was introduced to the grandeur of some ancient mountain ranges. Rocks, whose colours range from red and orange through to yellow and purple, as the sun moves across the hot land creating a landscape that excites the spirit. You feel as if you want to sit and listen to the quietness, just knowing that it has been there forever. The prehistoric nature of this place stirs long forgotten memories in the heart.

The land almost speaks to you as you recognise how eons of seasons have washed this land, until just the bare rocks are left as testimony to what must have been in the past. Yet one shower of rain transforms this place into a tapestry of colour, as the wildflowers bloom for their short lifespan, before dropping their seeds in wait for the next rain. A living desert that languishes in the hot sun waiting for moisture to bring it back to life.

A desert that has seen many changes both within its own structure and the people who walk its pathways. An ancient landscape that seems almost burdened with memories of the past, yet if you close your eyes and listen with your heart, you can sense what has been before.

Standing on a rocky outcrop we could see for miles. The small township where my son lives, the surrounding hills, and the tracks leading in many different directions placed there for man's convenience. Last night there had been rain and the waterholes were full, and the native children were noisily enjoying the rare pleasure of swimming and splashing around. The usual reds and oranges were subdued by a haze of green as the new shoots were rapidly finding their way to the light.

Seeing the country transform before my eyes gave a clear image of how nature worked with the earth and the effect it had on all the living creatures. An overview of how dependant each is on the other and the effect they all have on the total picture. The land, its people, the wildlife and the constantly changing seasons. All leave their mark.

Man's influence was evidenced by the roads, townships, mining activities and pastoral activities, and the scars that such occupation can leave. Even older evidence of man's presence was in rock paintings and bark stripped from the trees for everyday use. The landscape reflected when the earth had been respected and when it had not.

There was also evidence of earth movements and craters where meteorites had hit the earth in some distant past. All were there to be seen as a statement of what had gone before. The land was still beautiful, however, it was testimony to all it had experienced and endured.

I was reminded that our own journey reflects the many changes we have undergone, and that when we are nearing the completion of our learning then we, too, would reflect the sum total of our experiences. We would be able to look at ourselves and see the evidence of the splendour and the moments of disrespect.

When I came back into the township I still had that panoramic view in my mind whilst interacting with the people around me. Seeing everything close up, I became aware of how all the pieces of everyday life fit into the greater scheme of things.

Often we get so caught up in the details that we forget what the overview looks like and where all the bits and pieces fit in. Sometimes we need to take time out to view the big picture, otherwise we can become bogged down in the physical and materialistic details of every day existence, convinced that this is all there is to life. Then we become judgemental because we have not taken the time to step back and seek another viewpoint.

Belief systems are like that; we get so caught up in the truth of our belief so that we prevent ourselves from seeing the big picture. Our negative emotions and beliefs are like the scars upon the landscape.

'Jill' came to see me about all the problems she was having in her life. She had enormous difficulties in letting people get close to her and was suffering from panic attacks and bouts of extreme sadness. It was affecting her health and her employment.

She had a history of experiencing situations where people she loved most either hurting her or abandoning her. Her last experience was her husband having an affair with her best friend. She was frightened to let people get too close because she did not want to experience any more hurt, and had reached the stage of being unable to trust people.

We spent a couple of sessions dealing with the betrayal by the husband and friend, and helping her to cope with her fears and sadness. Then her mother died suddenly whilst overseas and all the hurt and sadness returned.

We looked at her childhood and there did not seem to be any reason for inviting such betrayal and sadness into her life. She had always strived to be a 'good girl' but always seemed to be blamed for any wrong doing. She had an elder sister whom she loved but who did not have time for her. Throughout her childhood, she seemed to accept people's opinions when they suggested she was bad, and ignored the positive messages she received, particularly from her mother. It was as if she had come into this life prepared to believe everything bad about herself, although in essence she was a beautiful caring and loving woman.

Working through her grief I suddenly said to her, "You know it is almost as if you have been cursed". I'm not sure where the thought came from but I just felt the need to say it. However her response vindicated my impulsiveness. "I have been", was her calm reply. I was quite amazed at her calm acceptance of what I considered an outlandish statement and I queried as to why she believed she had been cursed.

She had spent some time in England whilst growing up and was walking through a market square one day when a gipsy just stopped her, put her hands gently on her shoulders, looked into her eyes and said, "My child, you have been cursed".

Well, a statement like that is going to leave its mark, and even if you did not believe in curses, the experience would certainly stay in your mind. I asked what the gipsy did next and she said she just walked away. She was too shocked to ask for any more information.

Whether she had been cursed or not was irrelevant. The thought had been put into her mind and therefore became a reality. We discussed how she felt about curses, and because of her cultural background where superstition was a part of life, curses were not too far removed from possibility.

However, she was eighteen when this happened and her experiences of loss and rejection had been happening even before this time. So, whatever belief was creating this situation in her life had to have been in place before then. I decided to do a past life reading to find out what belief system she had brought into this life with her.

It went back to a time when she was an Arab horseman taking part in a raiding party on a travelling family group in the desert. I picked up the life time as he was galloping towards an intended victim, an elderly woman dressed in black. She never wavered in her stance or stare as he thundered towards her with sword raised ready to decapitate. As the sword came down towards her neck, she fixed her gaze upon him, saying defiantly, "A curse upon you and all your people for all eternity". She was decapitated before he could pull the sword back, so the curse hung in the air to haunt him forever.

This type of curse is very powerful as it is impossible to do anything to the person who invoked the curse, as they are now dead. It is easy to accept the curse and it becomes part of the belief system. Because the curse was for, "..all eternity" it could not even be revoked at death because it has no ending. Being born into another life with that belief system would leave you very susceptible to hurt and punishment of some kind. Because the curse was non-specific then the punishment could take many forms.

Jill had reached this lifetime so fearful and convinced on the deeper level that she is going to experience loss and rejection, that she not only saw it where none existed, but also invited it into her life. This curse had become such a burden that she had reached the stage of having panic attacks and practically withdrawing from life itself.

It was interesting that she was told of this curse by just a stranger walking through the market place. It was almost as if her higher consciousness was presenting her with an opportunity to connect with this past and release the curse. Nothing happens by chance.

I asked her to forgive the Arab for the killing and hand the curse back to the old woman. However, she found his actions so abhorrent that she could not forgive him and felt that he deserved the curse. I had to find another way to help her release the hold this curse had on her.

We discussed at length that the Arab was caught up in that lifetime's drama of being the warrior and had been behaving in a way consistent with his culture and belief system.

It is important not to judge ourselves by our behaviour in another lifetime, we are just playing the role of that culture. It is not so important what we do, but it is important how we feel about what we have done.

If our behaviour is consistent with the times then there is a good chance that we will carry no guilt or negative 'baggage'. However, if we have judged our behaviour to be bad or have allowed another person's judgement to influence how we feel about our actions, then we will carry the guilt of that judgement. Guilt that will need to be addressed in another lifetime, guilt that will exist until we have forgiven ourselves.

We discussed the fact that the curse only existed today because the Arab accepted it and that we always have a choice as to whether to accept or reject another's opinion. His behaviour was consistent with the times and culture but the curse had been accepted, therefore the judgement was that he will now be punished. Jill's reluctance to forgive the Arab was based on the fact that she now judged his actions to be bad because they incurred a curse.

Jill came to realise that if she wanted to release the curse she would need to forgive him. I took her through a session of contacting the Arab and helped her to see him as just another aspect of herself working through life's lessons.

Her immediate impression of him was that he was ugly and fierce. We used a kite to release the guilt and the puppet to release the hold the curse had upon him. She then reported that he looked much better, and in fact, was really quite nice looking and gentle. Her perception of him was influenced by her judgement of him. Remove the judgement, and the perception alters.

I then asked her to visualise a cord connecting them representing the curse that had existed and had kept his lifetime alive for both of them. It was black and thick. She needed a sharp sword to cut the cord. I reminded her that it was a sword that started the curse, so it was appropriate that a sword should end the curse. She appreciated the significance and performed the surgery with pleasure. She was then able to forgive the Arab and release him to the light.

The curse had been like a scar upon her soul, reminding her of past judgements but never being able to be repaired. The Arab had given away his power to the curse, and therefore had been unable to remove it because he had no power over the curse.

In each subsequent lifetime there did not seem to be any reason for the punishment that was experienced, as they were only viewing the actions in relation to that lifetime. They could not see the big picture and how those actions related to another lifetime. They were caught up in the details.

An exercise I like to give my students is to imagine standing on a hilltop and seeing a river in the valley below. This lofty vantage point allows the whole river to be seen. From its simple origins you can see it flowing through the twists and turns as it meanders its way via narrow gorges and open planes to its final destination. A panorama giving an overview of the good times and the more difficult moments of its journey knowing that it ultimately reaches its destination.

However, if you imagine being down by the river you will notice that you can only see from the last bend to the next. You can assume that there is something before the last bend and there has to be something after the next bend because the river is flowing, but from your limited vision you do not know what has gone before or what lies ahead.

If we made all our decisions based on this limited vision then we would be denying ourselves the obvious benefits of being able to see the whole journey - the big picture. Yet, every time we take on a new lifetime it is like only being able to see that small section of the river, a section that may be anything from smooth and quiet to narrow and rushing over rocks. Yet even so, this river would represent only one of the journeys we travel.

Imagine a wheel with the spokes leading to the hub, and that the spokes represent the lessons we choose to learn. All our lessons are positive ones, and the spokes could represent such lesson paths as: love, forgiveness, acceptance, trust and compassion to name a few. On every one of those paths exists the opportunity to spend as many lifetimes as necessary to learn the lessons.

When looking at your river from the hilltop, you would be looking at only one of those spokes on the wheel. There are many other rivers representing all the lessons you have chosen to learn. If you are being affected by a past life, then it would be only those lifetimes that remain unresolved on this particular lesson path. We know what our lessons are by the challenges put across our path.

Often I am asked how many lifetimes a person has had, or how many they have left, however these questions are impossible to answer. One may be able to discover how many lifetimes a person has had on the particular lesson path they are on, but not how many lifetimes they have had in total. All the other lesson paths fade into the background when we incarnate into a life on a particular lesson path.

It is also impossible to determine how many lifetimes a person has left on their lesson path. It depends on how quickly they manage to learn the lesson and as they have free will this could be at any moment.

Another statement I often hear is that a person is on their last lifetime. Sounds very nice but this is something which is very difficult to ascertain whilst we are still alive. If that person does nothing before their death that incurs judgement of some kind, then they may be right. However, if they judge themselves to be guilty, for instance, and are unable to resolve it before they leave this lifetime, then they will probably need to come back to release the negativity.

If we can see that each lifetime is but an opportunity to learn a particular lesson then we are less likely to get caught up in the drama of life.

When we feel that each lifetime is all that we have then we are more likely to get caught up in self judgement.

So often our judgements are based on only what we perceive to be our truth, our belief of what is so. A belief and truth that is restricted by our limited vision, limited by our physical nature.

If looking at the big picture enables us to view without judgement, then that would also allow us to accept what is happening in our lives as part of the flow of life, not some external force interfering with us. We take back our personal power when we realise we always have a choice.

When we live without judgement then we are able to accept others and respect their right to pursue their own journey. What a peaceful place this would be if we could live with total acceptance.

Rise above the lower vibrations and look at your problems as a whole. See them with the eyes of a spirit, and you will be surprised how different they look.

7

Your Higher Consciousness

When we started dairy farming it did not take us long to realise that no matter how much we wanted the cows to perform in a certain way they would do exactly as they liked. True, you could train them to a milking pattern of twice a day and they would walk into the bales and stand to be milked. However, they would go in when they were ready and not before. They developed a real pecking order, the older ones more likely to be bossy putting the younger ones in their place.

You had the ones who liked to lead and those who insisted on going in last. They would just stand there chewing their cud, skilfully managing to work their way to the back of the yard and ignoring you completely. Then, when there were only a few of them left they would sedately walk in to the bale to be milked, calmly asserting their independence.

However, what really amazed me was that all the cows in the district would fall into an identical calving pattern. We would ring the farmer who was first to calve in the district and question him as to whether they were calving early or late and whether it was primarily a heifer or bull-calf drop. The other questions were usually about whether there were a lot of stillborn calves or twins. Believe it or not, whatever was happening on his farm would be what we would all experience.

The cows in the district seemed to have a group consciousness that influenced their calving patterns. They were responding to the weather conditions which determine if it is a year when there is likely to be plenty of feed or a shortage, feast or famine. They did not seem to realise that being on a farm, their feed was guaranteed. Their group consciousness took charge and dictated their calving pattern to ensure survival of the species.

It made me wonder if we have a group consciousness that affects our patterns of behaviour. Well, if we look at the labels we put on particular people then that may be how the group consciousness works. Like labelling the French as romantics and the Australians as laid back with a 'she'll be right mate' attitude. It is true that if you live in a country long enough you pick up the habits and mannerisms of its people, so that may well be the extent of group consciousness for humans.

So we must have an individual consciousness that attends to our survival needs like the group consciousness of the animals. A consciousness that knows what our higher purpose is and helps keep us on track. A consciousness that sees the big picture and does not get caught up in the details of day to day existence. A consciousness that attends to the survival needs of the spirit. A consciousness that is not restricted by the physical limitations of time and space, but is able to see what has gone before and what can come after where we are at any moment.

Time belongs to the physical and if we do not occasionally distance ourselves from time then the spiritual consciousness will create that space. How, you ask? By getting a cold, pulling a muscle, becoming stressed out and exhausted, losing your job - all of which force you to take a break. In extreme cases, you may even have an accident which will put you out of action for quite some time.

I was chatting to a colleague of mine, a psychologist, whom I had not seen for a few months. She was keen to tell me what had happened to her, knowing that I would appreciate it. She told me that she had been involved in a car accident six months previously, requiring hospitalisation for a month and several months in physiotherapy. She still had back pain to remind her of the accident.

I wondered what it was I was meant to appreciate, when she went on to explain, "I had been invited to attend a dream workshop in America and decided I could not go because my patients could not manage if I was away for a month. Then, just after I had declined the offer, I had this accident necessitating a month's stay in hospital".

She expressed how she should not have let her doubts and over concern for her patients stop her from doing something she really wanted to do. They managed quite well without her for the month, but she had not had the benefit of a pleasant break from routine and the experience of the workshop.

I laughed and said I did appreciate the irony of the situation. I asked her if she was able to go another time and she confirmed that was her intention. The back pain did go eventually after she sought help, and was completely gone by the time she went to America the following year.

My friend fully realised that the accident was not an accident but her higher consciousness telling her to take some time out for herself. She had been working long hours and had become so focused on her work and her patients that she was not finding time for herself. I saw her again after her return from America and she appeared extremely fit and well. She was now looking after herself and finding time to seek inner peace.

It really is a shame that we need to inflict such pain on ourselves to make ourselves stop and rest. I am guilty of the same behaviour. Some years ago I would not listen to my inner voice and ended up with acute sciatic pain to the point where I was hospitalised and put in traction for four days. The doctor thought it was a slipped disc and I came out worse than I went in because of his misdiagnosis. I also ended up in pain for about five weeks.

What did I need to learn? Well, for one thing the job I was in was not where I wanted to be, and also, that I should always listen to my inner voice. It's a shame it took five weeks for me to accept this lesson otherwise I could have been back on my feet much sooner. To be fair it is hard to think and focus when you are in severe pain. On the other hand, when I laid really still in bed the pain would stop, so I had plenty of time to contemplate my situation. Some of us are slow learners.

These situations happen when our higher consciousness, the part of us connected to our infinite nature, makes a decision on our behalf. When caught up in the details of every day life our higher consciousness can see when we are losing the plot. An accident or something similar makes us stop and take notice. Something makes us take time out to reassess our situation. If we assumed that our waking conscious state is the only time we make decisions then we are denying ourselves the opportunity to see things from another perspective.

'Clare' came to see me because she was concerned about her health. She had a history of suffering from chronic illness over many years. She always felt unwell and constantly came down with minor infections. She was now diagnosed with chronic fatigue syndrome.

Clare had spent her whole life doing what her parents wanted her to do. She had done well at school, gone on to university and completed the course of her parent's choice. She was now an accountant and very good at what she did. However, she was not happy and ended up being sick all the time. It was becoming a problem for herself and her employers so she decided to take time out to think about her future.

Using a long holiday to think about her life she came back determined to be true to herself. She really wanted to be an artist and work with her creative instincts. This was her love and she felt really good about herself when immersed in her art. But, she was concerned that her parents would not approve of her choice of lifestyle, and regard her education as a waste of time and money.

Her higher consciousness had created the bouts of illness in an endeavour to force Clare to reassess her way of life. She ignored the messages until she become so debilitated that she had to leave work just to get through each day. Chronic fatigue syndrome is very much a condition of today's lifestyle. It is our present culture of constant hard work without paying attention to our spiritual, emotional and mental needs that has necessitated the creation of a condition that makes us take a rest.

I discussed with Clare the need to put her back in charge of her life so that she no longer needed to resort to conditions such as chronic fatigue syndrome.

Using images of her parents controlling her by pulling attached strings, I guided her to cut those strings to liberate herself. I then gave her the image of putting her back in charge of her life. The image I like to use for this belief is a control panel - where she can sit and press the right buttons to redirect her life.

This is a very powerful image, and it is amazing how often people will tell me that there is somebody else sitting at their control panel. Quite often it is a partner, parent, boss or some other dominant person in their life. Occasionally, it is some unknown dark cloaked person representing their fears or a belief that they are controlled by outside forces. In these instances, it is important to evict the intruder and place themselves at their own control panel. A very powerful visual image for the subconscious mind to store in its data bank, reaffirming who is in control.

When we believe we are not in control then our belief system must have somebody or something else in control. This belief or assumption then places us at a disadvantage and we feel vulnerable. When we feel vulnerable then our self-confidence is affected and we undermine our purpose and trust in ourselves. This is when we start to rewrite the script.

Negative belief systems are created by negative emotions and these have an impact, not only on our journey and learning, but also the physical conditions we invite into our life. When we cherish and love something then we do all in our power to protect, nurture and care for the object of our respect. However, when we hold something in low esteem then we do not care for it in the same way. In fact we often neglect it entirely, sometimes wishing to hurt or dispose of it in some manner.

If these negative emotions and beliefs are behind the scripts that we write, then it would be easy to see how we could invite physical conditions into our life that are designed to punish, hurt and frighten us in some way. The emotion or belief would determine what we include in the script of our life's performance. These are often the physical conditions we bring into life with us as congenital conditions or birth defects.

However, what about the conditions we create during our lifetime. Conditions that we may have included after we started our life's journey. Are they preventable, are they curable, are they necessary? It's only when we allow ourselves to peruse the script that we can answer those questions, and we do that by meditating and being in touch with our higher consciousness - looking at the big picture. Or taking time out to just sit and think whilst enjoying a moment of solitude.

Sometimes that is not easy as we usually choose to meditate or seek solitude only when we are anxious or concerned about something. Anxiety causes static in the airways and then seeking answers becomes more difficult. When we are calm and not stressed we do not think about contacting our higher consciousness as there does not seem to be a reason to do so, yet that would be the best time. We can be contrary creatures sometimes.

When the spirit is in disharmony it will reflect on the physical eventually. This may take five minutes, five years or five thousand years, but if the negative belief system is not addressed then somewhere, sometime, it will present itself in the physical. We can ignore it and suppress it but eventually it will show itself. This can apply not only to physical ailments, but behaviour patterns and attitudes.

However, if we look at the physical manifestations we have created we can usually work out what negative belief system is at work. Once we isolate the belief system then we can change it and consequently remove the need to create that physical condition again.

As a rough rule of thumb the part of the body affected can give you a general indication of what belief system is creating the condition.

The Body

If we look at the body as a whole it is made up of billions of smaller structures all of which are available to vent our negative beliefs. We are made up of cells, tissues, organs and systems.

When our cells are affected we are attacking the building blocks and maintenance team. The tissues are our communication and integration specialists, whereas the organs are the production team. Our systems assume the management role. All can be sabotaged with equal effect.

When we create conditions that attack the function of the cells, such as growths and wasting then this is a reflection of change at the deepest level possible. We are destroying the building blocks of our life and preventing positive regrowth and maintenance. Beliefs that we are not worthy to continue living, are often behind such conditions.

When the tissues are involved then we are interfering with our ability to communicate, either stuck in the past or unable to move forward. Beliefs that we are not worthwhile are usually behind these types of breakdown.

When an organ is affected then the negative belief system has reached a stage where production has been curtailed or stopped completely. Several different negative beliefs are usually at work here involving a loss of purpose or direction.

If a whole system breaks down then the cells, tissues and organs are all involved and the level of disharmony cannot be ignored. Negative beliefs have been harboured for so long that they are now affecting the management level. Negative beliefs of hopelessness and despair are usually behind total collapse of a system.

The Skeletal System

The skeletal system represents support and whenever we believe support is withdrawn then this will be reflected in the bones and joints. If you lose your job or business has become slow, then fear of losing physical means of support will create problems within the spine, or muscles associated with the spine.

Alternatively if you feel trapped in a situation or unable to make decisions, then the fear of moving will create problems in the hips and legs. Quite often when overburdened with responsibilities (real or imagined) the body will create difficulties across the shoulders and upper arms. Lower arms and hands are associated with touching and holding, and respond negatively to beliefs that you cannot trust yourself. Inflexible attitudes reflect in neck and ankle problems - the two areas of the skeletal system which demand the greatest flexibility and strength.

The Nervous and Endocrine System

The nervous system together with the endocrine system is part of the communication and control function of the body. When these parts of the body are affected then usually it is responding to an underlying belief of an inability to communicate, not being in control of your life or feelings of being out of balance.

Stuttering is a condition of the nervous system, and the ability to communicate is severely limited. Nervous conditions are a response to beliefs that you are not in control of your life or direction. Skin is one of the sense organs and will respond by protecting itself if the belief system is one of being controlled by others. Psoriasis and other skin eruptions are a normal protective response.

Hormonal conditions will reflect feelings of separation, being not unified or integrated, that the system has let you down. They indicate a belief that you have no confidence in your own abilities.

The Cardiovascular and Lymphatic System

The cardiovascular and lymphatic system are involved in transportation, both delivery and elimination, and are therefore very involved in keeping everything on the move. The heart is the pump that keeps the transportation system going and is considered so important that the developing embryo's heart is formed and beating four weeks after fertilisation.

Heart and circulatory problems reflect an underlying belief system indicating that there is no joy left in life and living itself and just being alive has become a burden. Weak or blocked arteries reflect that the purpose of living has become obscure or lost or you are resisting or rejecting the path you are on. Whenever life is considered not worth living, then there is no joy or purpose left and your heart and cardiovascular system will be affected.

The lymphatic system does not have a pump like the heart and relies on movement to aid its transportation purpose of circulating tissue fluids, proteins and fats. This systems plays an important role in the defence of the body against infections. Defence of the self is a reflection of personal self-esteem. If you do not like yourself or lack self-respect then the desire to protect yourself must be diminished.

Problems within the lymphatic nodes come from blame or feelings of not being good enough. The tonsils will be affected when judging yourself or voicing self disapproval. Thymus problems arise when you feel threatened by others and you do not believe you are capable of protecting yourself. The spleen will respond to feelings of hate for yourself or the way your life is heading.

The Respiratory System

The respiratory system allows us to absorb oxygen into the bloodstream, remove carbon dioxide, filter, warm and humidify the air we breathe - through the simple technique of inhaling and exhaling.

Disharmony within the respiratory system reflects a deep sense of fear about life and living.

The first thing we do when we are frightened is to stop breathing - hold our breath. If we are frightened to speak out, our larynx and pharynx go into spasm and create a feeling of tightness in the throat. The lump in the throat is also evident when suddenly frightened or overwhelmed by emotion. When the belief is that things are getting on top of you, or you are frightened of not being able to cope, an upper respiratory tract infection will occur - the common cold.

The lungs are affected by deep feelings of foreboding or grief. Breathing becomes shallow during depression or when life's energy is depleted. Bronchial problems will be created when frightened by what life is offering you - fear of breathing in life.

The Digestive System

The digestive system is all about assimilation and elimination. We take in what we need and eliminate what we no longer require. Conditions that affect the digestive system will have a direct relationship to beliefs involving the assimilation of new ideas, accepting them into your reality, or the letting go of what is not longer needed.

Any fear of change will show up in liver conditions; the seat of transformation. The gall bladder can respond negatively when accumulating old hurts and perceived injustices. The pancreas, because of its ability to aid the acceptance of nutrients and conversion of sugar to energy is affected when the sweetness in life is no long perceived.

Stomach conditions are negative responses to new concepts, beliefs or emotions. The body responds to 'gut feelings', therefore is susceptible to feelings of fear and anger. It must store what we are being asked to accept - rejection causes disharmony.

Small intestine problems are related to the assimilation of all learning that comes our way. You will notice that people may get intestinal problems during times of stress, for example when undertaking examinations of any kind. This is a challenge to the acceptance of learning.

The large intestine deals with the elimination of what we no longer require. Problems in this area have a direct relationship to holding onto the past. Obsession with possessions and a lack of personal security can often lead to bowel problems. Constipation represents a need to hang on at all costs.

The Urinary System

The urinary system eliminates excess fluids and waste whilst maintaining electrolyte and acid-base balance. The kidneys and excretory system are important in maintaining balance of essential blood constituents.

If the kidneys are affected in a negative way they are probably responding to underlying belief systems involving needs as opposed to wants. Our wants are often in excess of our needs.

Fluid retention often reflects our inability to release fears of not having enough. Kidney stones are lumps of unresolved anger or bitterness usually about not getting what you want. Kidney failure is reflecting the child within us all that sits and sulks at not getting what it wants.

Bladder problems are a reflection of emotional annoyance. Water represents our emotions, and if passing water is a problem, then dealing with people who really annoy you is an issue you are reluctant to confront. *Micturition,* frequent urination, is a feeling of being out of touch with those around you, or not in control of your emotions. Bed wetting is a fear of someone close to you, often a parent, resulting in hanging on during the daytime.

The Reproduction System

Reproduction of the species is one of the most important aspects of survival and humans are no exception. Survival is dependent on cell reproduction and within every cell is the blueprint for another enabling cells to reproduce themselves when their life is no longer functional.

When the sperm and ovum come together a new and unique package of genetic material comes into being, reflecting the blueprints from two different individuals. The male reproductive system is designed to produce sperm and impregnate a female to continue the species. The female reproductive system is designed to produce ovum, nurture and feed the new embryo until birth, then feed the new human baby until it can digest nutrients of more substance than milk. Totally different roles and responsibilities.

In the same way that the cell reproduces itself, we wish to do the same. However, in humans, emotions are involved in the bringing together of the sperm and the ovum. Consequently, problems arising in the reproductive system have a strong connection to relationship difficulties, self-identity problems and fears about sexuality.

Conditioning from our childhood, (both parental and cultural,) positive and negative experiences through our formative years, and belief systems brought in with us, all contribute to our perceptions of our sexuality and our ability to relate to others. Disharmony within the reproductive system will reflect these perceptions.

Breast cancer is often a resentment factor relating to the mother; she suckled you at the breast. Fibroids and tumours can reflect resentment towards partners who have hurt your feminine image.

Menstrual problems are reflections of negative attitudes towards one's own femininity or a desire to flush away guilt feelings about sex and the genitals. Often reflecting a sense of not being loved for oneself. Frigidity and impotence are expressions of sexual guilt and/or self-image problems reflecting a desire not to reproduce the self or self-rejection.

Prostate and menopause problems can reflect negative beliefs about getting older and not accepting the natural flow of life.

Our thoughts and beliefs are the force behind our reality. If disharmony on any level has entered into your life, then you can change it by changing the negative belief system that has created that reality. Remove the scars and evidence of disrespect from your landscape.

We are never out of control of our lives, we just lose sight of the big picture and allow the details of everyday living to influence our belief about our reality. We lose the plot.

However, all is not lost. We simply re-write the script to bring us back to our original story line and then we will be back on track again. Empowered to be ourself again. Self-empowerment.

*It is time to discard
the bondage your have
placed yourself in,
discard the chains
and see yourself as you
truly are.
Allow yourself to be
uplifted.
It matters not how
difficult your path,
seek only the light.
Be lifted as on eagles
wings to your higher
realms.*

8

The Magic of Colour

The sun had come out as a shower of rain was gently washing the grass and plants that flourish in our garden. It was as if they were opening themselves up for this cleansing bath, and allowing the drops to wash away the dust that collected after several warm and windy days. You could almost hear a collective cry of delight as the rain brought a sense of renewal and the colours appeared far more vibrant.

However, it was the rainbow with its myriad of colours that had appeared with the sun that really caught my eye. The stories told by my Irish grandfather came back about the leprechaun's promise of the pot of gold at the rainbow's end. That optimistic thought that if you keep going and searching you will get your reward.

Colour has always interested man and has often been the tool for communication and symbolism. All cultures right from our distant past to today, have used the natural colours found in plants and the soil for painting their bodies, abodes, spiritual icons, adornments, clothing and utensils. Colour has always attracted us and has the ability to excite, stimulate, sedate or calm us in its various hues. What is it about colour that can influence such a variety of responses?

If we consider that everything has energy and vibrates at unique frequencies, then colour itself must have energies and vibrations that connect with our own energies, urging us to respond in some manner. We even give colour meaning through our language, "I've got the blues", "I'm green with envy", "I see red when I feel cheated", "I'm in the pink", or "I'm in a black mood today". We all understand what people mean when they relate it to colour. People even talk about red cars going faster and the safest vehicles on the road are yellow and white. They even quote statistics. However, the reason for these figures are that the drivers respond to the colour of the car they are driving.

We respond differently to various colours and hues. Interior decorators use colour to create the impression of warmth or coolness, depending on which way a house is facing. Many public buildings and institutions use colour to enhance their purpose, for instance hospitals and schools.

If we wanted to enhance our purpose then we should use colour to help us on our journey. However, colour is often an indicator of what is happening on a deeper level of our consciousness. A reflection of our underneath belief system. The colours we are attracted to, and those we have an aversion to, are often an indication of both what we are working with and perhaps the changes we are rejecting. It may be worth looking at those colours we like, to see if we are utilising their benefits or using them as a crutch. Alternatively, looking at the colours we do not like, may help to establish whether they are not what we need, or indicate if we are rejecting the opportunity to change a belief system. One that has been operating for some time and has become familiar.

When working with my clients, I often note what they are wearing to see if they are conducive to change, or are stuck in their negative belief system. The clothes we buy are often an indication of what we are feeling. It is a really good exercise to open the wardrobe doors and stand back and just look at the mix of colours. Are they primarily of one colour or do they fall within a narrow colour range? Those colours are the ones you are attracted to at the moment and are a reflection of either what you are feeling or what changes you are currently undergoing.

I have been attracted to colour for as long as I can remember, so when introduced to the concept that colour can influence us, then I looked at its ability to help us heal ourselves. I gradually developed a love of colour and how to use it to help us change our negative belief systems. My meditation tapes are designed to gently guide people into creating positive change by the use of colour. In my therapy, I also use colour as an integral part of the healing process.

Colour is available to everybody and does not have to be purchased. I believe it is there for us to use for both creative and healing purposes. A healing gift that has perhaps been ignored for many years. We can use meditation to bring colour into our lives by imagining that we are being given coloured balls of light by the healing masters of the universe. This is a meditation I use on one of my tapes.

However, you can also influence change by bringing colour into your every day life by either wearing the colour that you need or introducing it into your environment. You can do that with flowers, cushions, pictures on the wall or decorative glass that reflects the light. These are just some suggestions; you may have other favourite ways of introducing colour. You are limited only by your imagination. I often suggest to my clients that if colour they need is perhaps a colour they are not comfortable wearing, that they buy underwear of that colour. That makes them laugh but it does bring the vibrations of that colour closer to the skin!

To understand in which way colour can help change the belief systems then perhaps we need to explore what gift each colour brings into our lives.

Use the suggested visualisations within a white light meditation, adding the colour or colours you may need to your body. I like to use small swatches of coloured felt in the different hues to reflect which energy I wish to invite into my life. If you have a physical condition you wish to help, then place the appropriate coloured swatch on the area that is affected, or alternatively on the chakra that works with that part of the body. You can do both if you wish. I will include at the end of this chapter a suggested white light meditation that you can use to integrate the visualisations suggested.

Red:

Wonderful colour of strength, courage, confidence, purpose and direction. Helps restore energy and vigour wherever that is missing in your life. Physically helps with leg, knee and feet problems. Very grounding colour if you are feeling scattered or lost.

Red is the colour of the base chakra, an energy centre, which is located at the base of the spine. You can use colour to balance these energy centres by either placing colour swatches over that area or visualising drawing colour into that chakra.

When my students have difficulty staying focused, or fall asleep during the meditations, I put red socks on them. That keeps them tuned in. I also use this colour if a client feels they have no control over their life or feel disempowered.

Red socks or red underwear are very empowering as are red slacks or a red shirts. In the house, red flowers or eating red vegetables can help create significant change.

Use this colour in conjunction with visualisations of cutting the puppet strings that you have allowed others to pull. Alternatively, see yourself at your control panel or if you feel trapped, visualise removing the shackles around your ankles.

Orange:

A vibrant colour that stimulates and clarifies. A colour that is a mixture of red and yellow, two of the primary colours, and therefore contains the energies of both these colours. Every decision we make has an impact on our relationships, whether these be family, intimate, career, community or global. Making decisions is something we are faced with every day and sometimes these are easy and other times we continue to procrastinate.

Orange helps clarify the mind, enabling us to make the decisions that are in our best interests on all levels of our consciousness - mind, body and spirit. Physically helps with reproduction problems.

Orange is the colour of the naval chakra which is located just below your navel. Use this colour to balance and harmonise this chakra which will help restore balance in your relationships.

When next confronted with a decision, whether it be in the home, work or community environment, bring the colour orange into the discussion and you will assist the decision making process and reduce the tendency towards procrastination. I often suggest to business men that they introduce orange flowers into board meetings to stop the waffle. Also useful at school committee meetings or family discussions.

If making decisions is a problem for you, or

your relationships are suffering because of indecision, bring orange into your life in the many different ways available to you. Allow yourself to listen to your inner voice. The clarity will be there and will come in the form of inspiration or just awareness. An excellent visualisation for this colour is to see yourself on your path in life, confronted by a fork in the road and being able to choose which path to take with confidence.

Yellow:

Who cannot be happy when surrounded by yellow - a happy and optimistic colour. The colour of sunshine and gold. A colour to make you smile. Yellow encourages the feeling of wanting to get on with life. Very empowering.

Yellow is the colour of the solar plexus chakra which is the located just above the naval. The area of our gut feelings, where we first generate anger and fear. It is also the area of assimilation, the taking in of new ideas. Any problems with digestion or elimination are assisted by the introduction of yellow into your personal environment.

When we are frightened of change or learning something new, then yellow is what we need to introduce into our life. So often we get caught up in the drama of every day life and are unable to move on or let go of the past. Yellow inspires optimism and the promise of wonderful new opportunities. We get caught up in doing the same things over and over again and not able to break the repetitive behaviour patterns.

Introduce yellow into your life in any way that appeals to you. A great visualisation for breaking free of the past is to imagine that you are stuck on a big wooden treadmill going around and around. Then imagine just getting off and burning the treadmill. Wonderful statement for the subconscious mind to assimilate.

Green:
Why do you think hospitals use green? Because it is a wonderful healing colour, the colour of the heart chakra. A colour to soothe and bring peace to the heart and soul. A colour that is a combination of blue and yellow and contains the energies of both those colours.

If healing is what you need at this time, then green is the colour you need around you. The world is full of green through our plants and trees. The forests of the world are places of great healing if we would but take the time to avail ourselves of their wonderful energies.

Overcoming sadness, loss and grief is one of our biggest lessons in life and green is the colour to help us through these difficult times. I love to use green in my healing sessions as people respond with such joy when they allow themselves to soak up its energy. From a physical point of view, heart and lung problems respond well to the inclusion of the colour green.

If one of your belief systems is that you need to suffer or deserve punishment of some kind, then green is the colour to help you forgive yourself and restore your harmony.

One of the visualisations I like to use for forgiveness is to imagine seeing an image of yourself before you and offer green balls of light to the image. Once this has been accepted, then offer a bunch of violets as a symbol of forgiveness. Then give your image a hug offering love and forgiveness. This a very powerful message for your soul.

Blue:
Wonderful colour of expression and creativity. Whenever we think about landscapes we include the colour blue into our picture, whether it be sky or sea. Blue surrounds us and inspires us.

Blue is the colour of the throat chakra and is the seat of our creativity. We are constantly creating either by speaking our truth, writing how we feel or making something to express our intentions.

So often we feel gagged and unable to say what we wish to say, either through fear of offence or reprisal. These fears stifle our creativity and stop us from achieving our goals in life. If we are blocked in one area of expression then all the others are affected to some degree. Physically, blue is wonderful for throat, ear, nose, arm and hand problems.

If your belief system is that you have nothing of value to offer the world, then introducing blue into your life with help restore your faith in yourself. We are all unique and beautiful individuals, however, through conditioning or experience, we allow ourselves to devalue our true worth.

A wonderful visualisation for this belief system is to swim in a beautiful blue lake to wash away all the fears. Then imagine walking into a beautiful white building which has pictures hanging on the wall. These pictures represent all the times you have condemned yourself and put yourself down. Imagine removing these pictures and taking them outside and burning them. Then go back inside the building and put up pictures of yourself of times when you felt really good about yourself. A strong message of reaffirming to yourself your true worth.

Indigo:

This magical colour which is a combination of blue and violet conjures up illusion and imagery. A colour that connects your creative genius with your higher self. Perception and inner vision are the gifts of this marvellous colour. It's no wonder that spiritually involved people and those referred to as clairvoyant, often wear indigo or violet as these colours encourage 'clear vision' and connection with the higher self.

Our perception is influenced by our belief systems and personal experiences. We often see what we expect to see or what we believe we will see. You only have to talk to police officers who take statements to realise that everybody has their own version of what happened.

Indigo is the colour of the third eye chakra located between the eyebrows, and physically relates to the eyes and mind. Any problems with the eyes, stress related problems and anxiety will respond really well to indigo.

If one of your belief systems has created doubts in your life or led you to believe that you have no intuition, or ability to see things as they really are, then you perhaps need to introduce indigo into your life in some manner.

One of my favourite visualisations for perception and inner vision is to imagine yourself standing under a waterfall allowing the water to wash away all doubts and fears. Then imagine going to a part of the river that is wide and still. In this part of the river there are some large rocks that are stopping you seeing clearly to the bottom. These rocks represent the fears and anxieties that you have allowed to cloud your vision and connection with your higher self. Remove the rocks and allow them to be taken away by one of your guides or angels. Then look again into the river and see the bottom clear and clean. You can decorate the bottom with something beautiful if you like.

This is a clear message to your subconscious mind that you are now ready to see clearly and are prepared to move confidently into the future.

Violet:

Faith, belief in oneself and forgiveness are some of the attributes of this inspirational colour. Connection with your higher self and universal consciousness is aided by this colour which has been used by kings and spiritual leaders for most of our known history.

Violet is the colour of the crown chakra located on the top of the head. Physically this colour assists in confusion, dementia, delusions and despair.

Sometimes we lose faith in our abilities or lose a sense of our own identity. Confusion about who we are or why we are here, or feelings of hopelessness and "what's the use" are all aided by the colour violet. Belief systems that infer that you are unforgivable often lead to feelings of despair and hopelessness. Feelings of being unforgivable are the most difficult to overcome without help of some kind. If we truly believe that we are unforgivable then that is tantamount to saying there is no hope, whereas we are all forgivable.

There is nothing that you have done, and I mean absolutely nothing, that cannot be forgiven. However, if you are wanting somebody else's forgiveness then you have totally disempowered yourself. The forgiveness you seek is your own and only you can give it to yourself. Take this moment now to decide to forgive yourself for whatever it is that you have judged to be unforgivable, and let it go. Nothing is worth total condemnation. You are a beautiful energy of light and love that deserves to be loved and nurtured.

The introduction of violet in its many forms will assist in the reversal of this belief system and assist in the forgiveness of the self.

A visualisation I encourage, with the use of violet to help with all these negative beliefs, is to imagine that you are in a dark hole, almost like a void, and that there is just a pin-hole of light far above you. Focus on this light and imagine reaching out your hands and feeling a ladder in front of you. Climb the ladder, still focused on the light above you, allowing yourself to get closer and closer until you are completely in the light. Then fill in the black hole you have just climbed out of, first with violet light then white light. Bathe in the white light until all the negative feelings have been washed away.

Then take the time to create a beautiful environment for yourself where you can feel at home and at peace. Allow yourself to feel your angels and guides around you offering love and support.

An extremely effective message to the subconscious mind to let it know that you have restored your belief in yourself and that you are now back on track.

White Light Meditation:

Relax in a comfortable place where you will not be disturbed. Close your eyes and take a deep breath in; breath out and relax. Repeat this twice more allowing yourself to relax more and more.

Visualise yourself within the glow of the beautiful white light, that is the source of divine love. Allow this beautiful light to filter through you, letting it permeate every cell in your body, every part of you. If you find it difficult to let the light move through certain parts of your body then you may be holding some negativity there. Just let the light gently wash away the blockage until it is able to move throughout your whole being without hindrance. Allow the peace that this white light cleansing brings to reach your whole consciousness; mind, body and spirit.

Then allow yourself to be drawn up into that light, higher and higher until you reach a place of pure golden light. A place of such peace and harmony that you feel very safe, very comfortable.

When you reach this very safe place allow yourself to do the visualisations suggested, followed by drawing in a big ball of coloured light that corresponds with the visualisation used. You can combine the visualisations if you wish to work on a couple of areas at the same time.

When you have finished. bring yourself back to your full consciousness by filling your whole body with the colours you have used and moving each part of your body as the colour is accepted.

If you feel you need more direction, then record on tape a meditation using the suggestions and visualisations given above. Sometimes your own voice can be the most empowering tool you can use to communicate with your subconscious mind. Alternatively you may wish to use one of the meditation tapes I have released, including a white light meditation with colour.

Putting you back in charge of your life is the most important thing you can do for yourself. Self-empowerment is your most precious state of reality. We can take back our power as easily as we give it away. The chance is here now to reassert your power over yourself. Please take a moment to consider. As always, the choice is yours.

9

Self Empowerment

"We must have a name" was the insistent call from my students. They were attending the last two sessions of their studies and had almost completed all the requirements to obtain their diploma. This was the last time they would all be together and they were feeling a little sad. However, their main concern was that they wanted a name for the therapy I had been teaching them.

They had spent the previous eighteen months

attending the workshops, practicing in groups, attending assessments and completing their case studies and thesis. They were on the brink of becoming practitioners and they were now demanding a label for the healing tools they had been given. I acknowledged that they had a point and that perhaps we needed to give 'it' an image.

I asked them to leave it with me overnight whilst I meditated on an appropriate name that would embody the therapy. Very difficult, considering that 'it' is a compilation of what I have been taught and what I have added to the therapy through my own discoveries. 'It' did not fit into any specific category as 'it' used several tools, added the dynamics of imagery and, through an understanding of the workings of the mind, allowed change to happen immediately. 'It' did not conform to any specific modality.

During that night I found myself awake at two in the morning, as is normal when my guides want to talk to me. I was aware of many thoughts going around in my head. My guides have found that two in the morning is a good time to talk to me as I am a captive audience. This time I had inadvertently invited their interruption to my sleep as I had promised my students I would have an answer in the morning. You would think I should have known better. Never mind, it was for the best really. Who needs sleep?

They took me on a journey that highlighted all the times I had listened to my inner voice and their guidance. All the times I had instinctively used something different in my therapy with wonderful results. The incredible images they had shown me to help so many clients, and the power of using images. How all that I had taught my students I had learnt through just trusting my instincts and remembering the thought behind the images used.

I was shown the colours and how I had come to appreciate their healing qualities and how they brighten up our lives and creative spirit.

They also reminded me of the spiritual lessons I had learnt and continue to learn. The timelessness of emotions and how we can carry belief systems from one lifetime to another. The destructive nature of negative emotions and beliefs, and how we can change our whole perception by changing the belief.

They inspired me to make three homoeopathic plant essences without really knowing what they were for beforehand. The essences that assist the three stages of healing: integration, transformation and acceptance. **Integration**, the first stage of healing where we need to recognise we have a condition that needs to change. **Transformation**, the second stage of healing where no matter what healing is needed we must move from where we are to where we want to be. **Acceptance,** the final stage of healing where we must accept the healing for it to become our reality.

So often we seek help from different people and use many different remedies, but until we accept the healing it has not happened. This may seem a simple observation but it is the acceptance that the negative belief system has finally been changed to a positive belief that completes the healing.

They also showed me how these essences could be used in conjunction with other remedies or methods of treatment. Plant essences that are non-specific and can therefore be used in any healing situation whether it be for a physical, mental, emotional or spiritual condition of disharmony. An integrated healing essence that could be integrated into daily life.

Sometimes we need to be reminded of how far we have come to realise that change has taken place. I was reminded of the many lessons I had learnt and how I had included them in my everyday life. I kept hearing the word integrated.

I was then reminded of what the basis of my therapy was all about: self-empowerment. The mind is a powerful friend, but can be a powerful enemy is a powerful friend, but can be a powerful enemy when the belief systems encourage sabotage of our good intentions. To change the negative belief system is to take, back control of yourself and remove the hidden saboteurs. When we are in charge of ourselves then we are self-empowered.

My guides reminded me of the various methods I had devised to help people take back control, and how this had changed their lives. I was reminded of the joy I experienced in seeing somebody walk out of my consultation room with a smile on their face and a lightness in their walk. The satisfaction it gave me to help these people take back their power.

This is what my therapy and my teaching is all about - putting the power back into their hands, hearts, minds and souls. My therapy is an integrated self-empowerment therapy. I finally had a name for my students, a name that summarises what it is that we do. ISET - Integrated Self-empowerment Therapy. It was now four in the morning and I could finally get some sleep before commencing my full day's teaching in a few hours time.

My students were delighted as they felt it embraced the spirit as well as the essence of the therapy. They were now excited at the tools they had to offer their clients, and that the therapy now had an identity. It is my pleasure to teach and pass on to others the ability to create positive change in a safe and nurturing way. I offer this opportunity to create change in your own life and take back your power. Enjoy the journey towards your own self-empowerment.

It is only six years since I opened my centre and so much has changed in those few years. Moving rapidly from just a therapy centre to a teaching institution as well. I am always amazed at how much change one can invite into one's life once the saboteurs have been removed.

However, one belief that I treasure is that I have total free will and I always have a choice.

So do you.

About the Author

Eileen Goble was born in England and lived there until her family migrated to Australia when she was ten. She lives in Melbourne with her husband, has four children, two grandchildren and a spoilt dog called Harry.

Growing up in an Irish catholic family she was exposed to a variety of spiritual messages from both her family and environment. It was very difficult to stay locked into one philosophy when surrounded by the myth, music and humour.

Some of her fondest memories are of listening to her grandfather telling stories of the 'little people', banshee and other mythological creatures. When the family gathered together there was always dancing, music and storytelling. Eileen's imagination was stimulated from a very young age. Accepting people as being fey and healing by touch was also part of her childhood background.

With such a convivial family it was an easy transition for Eileen to be always asking questions and seeking answers. This led her to be open and sensitive to energies and elements around her.

It was a natural progression for Eileen to become a writer and speaker when the time was right. She now delights in teaching and helping people find peace though self empowerment.